Cases in Emotional and Behavioral Disorders of Children and Youth

James M. Kauffman
University of Virginia

PEARSON

Merrill
Prentice Hall

Upper Saddle River, New Jersey
Columbus, Ohio

Library of Congress Cataloging-in-Publication Data

Kauffman, James M.
    Cases in emotional and behavioral disorders of children and youth / James M. Kauffman.
        p.   cm.
    Includes bibliographical references.
    ISBN 0-13-118567-5 (pbk.)
        1.   Behavior disorders in children—Case studies. 2. Adolescent psychopathology—Case
    Studies. 3. Mentally ill children—Case studies. I. Title.

    RJ506.B44K378 2005
    618.92′89—dc22   2003070767

Vice President and Executive Publisher: Jeffery W. Johnston
Acquisitions Editor: Allyson P. Sharp
Development Editor: Heather Doyle Fraser
Production Editor: Sheryl Glicker Langner
Design Coordinator: Diane C. Lorenzo
Cover Design: Thomas Borah
Cover Image: Corbis
Production Manager: Laura Messerly
Director of Marketing: Ann Castel Davis
Marketing Manager: Autumn Purdy
Marketing Coordinator: Tyra Poole

This book was set in Times Roman by Prentice Hall. It was printed and bound
by R. R. Donnelley & Sons Company. The cover was printed by The Lehigh Press, Inc.

Pearson Education Ltd.
Pearson Education Singapore Pte. Ltd.
Pearson Education Canada, Ltd.
Pearson Education–Japan

Pearson Education Australia Pty. Limited
Pearson Education North Asia Ltd.
Pearson Educación de Mexico, S.A. de C.V.
Pearson Education Malaysia Pte. Ltd.

10 9 8 7 6 5 4 3 2 1
ISBN: 0-13-118567-5

Preface

This casebook contains cases that I have garnered from my reading of both popular and professional literature and from personal contacts with individuals who have confronted difficult or disturbing behavior in their roles as parents, teachers, or adult members of a community. In some instances, I have used direct quotations from the source, sometimes with minor editing. In others I have summarized the original source in my own words. Still other cases were written by someone else, whom I credit as the source, specifically for this book. In all cases I have kept the facts conveyed by the original.

The cases are grouped by topic. However, instructors or students may find that a given case has conceptual links to more than one topic. This is as it should be, as emotional and behavioral disorders are not phenomena that can be packaged neatly into a single category.

Although the cases are grouped by specific topics, many or most of them could bear revisiting as a student progresses through coursework. Some of the questions about the cases, and some questions an instructor might want to ask or a student might pose, may have no fixed answer. Moreover, the "answers" might change after further study and research of the problem or topic area.

I have provided a brief introduction for each case. I have also suggested questions that could be discussed in class or answered in writing, or both. The questions I pose are by no means the only ones of importance, and I encourage instructors and/or students to formulate their own questions about the cases. If the source of the case is a published work, I give the citation and the full reference in the references for the casebook. If it was contributed by another individual or is based on my personal experience with students, I state that in the source note.

I hope this casebook will enrich and enliven any course in which it is used. It is important to recognize that all of the cases are descriptions of actual youngsters and events. They are not hypothetical. My hope is that studying them will help prepare the individuals who read them to work more effectively with young people who have such disorders.

James M. Kauffman
Charlottesville, Virginia – October, 2003

Discover the Companion Website Accompanying This Book

The Prentice Hall Companion Website: A Virtual Learning Environment

Technology is a constantly growing and changing aspect of our field that is creating a need for content and resources. To address this emerging need, Prentice Hall has developed an online learning environment for students and professors alike—Companion Websites—to support our textbooks.

In creating a Companion Website, our goal is to build on and enhance what the textbook already offers. For this reason, the content for each user-friendly website is organized by topic and provides the professor and student with a variety of meaningful resources. Common features of a Companion Website include:

For the Professor—

Every Companion Website integrates **Syllabus Manager™**, an online syllabus creation and management utility.

- **Syllabus Manager™** provides you, the instructor, with an easy, step-by-step process to create and revise syllabi, with direct links into Companion Website and other online content without having to learn HTML.

- Students may logon to your syllabus during any study session. All they need to know is the web address for the Companion Website and the password you've assigned to your syllabus.

- After you have created a syllabus using **Syllabus Manager™**, students may enter the syllabus for their course section from any point in the Companion Website.

- Clicking on a date, the student is shown the list of activities for the assignment. The activities for each assignment are linked directly to actual content, saving time for students.

- Adding assignments consists of clicking on the desired due date, then filling in the details of the assignment—name of the assignment, instructions, and whether or not it is a one-time or repeating assignment.

- In addition, links to other activities can be created easily. If the activity is online, a URL can be entered in the space provided, and it will be linked automatically in the final syllabus.

- Your completed syllabus is hosted on our servers, allowing convenient updates from any computer on the Internet. Changes you make to your syllabus are immediately available to your students at their next logon.

For the Student—

- **Introduction**—General information about the topic and how it will be covered in the website.
- **Web Links**—A variety of websites related to topic areas.
- **Timely Articles**—Links to online articles that enable you to become more aware of important issues in early childhood.
- **Learn by Doing**—Put concepts into action, participate in activities, examine strategies, and more.
- **Visit a School**—Visit a school's website to see concepts, theories, and strategies in action.
- **For Teachers/Practitioners**—Access information you will need to know as an educator, including information on materials, activities, and lessons.
- **Current Policies and Standards**—Find out the latest early childhood policies from the government and various organizations, and view state, federal, and curriculum standards.
- **Resources and Organizations**—Discover tools to help you plan your classroom or center and organizations to provide current information and standards for each topic.
- **Electronic Bluebook**—Paperless method of completing homework or essays assigned by a professor. Finished work can be sent to the professor via email.
- **Message Board**—Virtual bulletin board to post and respond to questions and comments from a national audience.

To take advantage of these and other resources, please visit the *Cases in Emotional and Behavioral Disorders of Children and Youth* Companion Website at

www.prenhall.com/kauffman

Contents

The Use of Cases

Cases have become an important teaching tool in many professional schools, including medicine, nursing, business, and, more recently, education. The basic idea is that students preparing to enter a given field can learn a great deal more by reading and thinking about actual problems than from reading the usual text material alone (Kauffman, Mostert, Trent, & Hallahan, 2002; Goor & Santos, 2002).

Cases usually are not meant to be used without a textbook that presents concepts in the typical expository or academic manner. Rather, they are meant to amplify concepts presented in a text, provide a scenario in which the concepts can be applied to real-life problems, and prompt deeper thinking and further questioning by students.

Of course, a case never provides all the information anyone could want or ask for. But in actual practice as well, professionals often must make judgments or decisions without having all the information they would like to have. Sometimes it is wise to wait for more information, but in some circumstances the practitioner cannot wait. Cases always demand that readers do two things: (a) make a judgment based on the information provided and (b) ask questions for which answers are not available. The following is always an important question: "What would you do, given the information we have?" However, another important question is: "Suppose we find out that _____, then what would you do?" The "Suppose. . . " requires asking additional questions in the light of what is already known about the case.

Instructors may use cases in a variety of ways. They may ask students to read a case and be ready to discuss it in class, to write answers to questions about the case, to pose additional questions about the case, or some combination of these or other tactics. The questions following each case are merely a beginning point for reflection on the meaning of the behavior described and the most appropriate way of responding to it.

1. Cases Illustrating the Nature of Emotional and Behavioral Disorders

Sometimes, we see rather clearly how adverse life circumstances can play a part in emotional or behavioral disorders. If we can put ourselves in the shoes of a child or youth, we might imagine how difficult it would be to cope with poverty, abuse, neglect, discrimination, failure, or other situations that we would have to overcome.

Tony

When he was 8, Tony Singleton [not his real name] was getting high on dope and booze he says he stole from his mother.

At 14, he was incarcerated after being convicted of breaking and entering, and petit larceny.

When, as a 17-year-old, he attacked two women near the University of Virginia, authorities decided juvenile court was no longer appropriate. And, in February, a Charlottesville Circuit judge sentenced 18-year-old Singleton to 11 years behind bars.

Court documents, based on statements by Singleton and interviews with people who have tried to help him, produce a picture of a troubled youth who throughout his short life has received services from an assortment of psychologists, social workers, probation officers, and teachers . . .

A psychiatric evaluation of Singleton prepared . . . by Park E. Dietz of the Forensic Psychiatry Clinic at the University of Virginia paints a portrait of a confused and desperate young man. Singleton told Dietz he was neglected by his mother, a local plant worker who was often away from home. She never married Singleton's father but lived with a succession of boyfriends, one of whom would regularly beat Singleton.

Singleton said his mother had . . . marijuana, and at a very young age he began to steal both [drugs] and money from her.

2

He said he sometimes smoked the dope. Other times he sold it to kids on the streets of Charlottesville.

[For two years], the . . . Social Services Department, which investigates complaints of abused and neglected children, received reports that Singleton, between 5 and 7 years old at the time, was not properly cared for.

A worker from the department observed that Singleton's mother left him free to roam. While unsupervised, he would break into cars and houses. Singleton was not properly dressed and occasionally slept outdoors.

Social workers arranged to have Singleton taken from his mother and placed with his paternal grandmother.

The grandmother lived in a three-bedroom house with 11 other people, including a mentally retarded daughter.

A probation officer who visited the home in 1983 described it: There was no front doorknob on the inside of the front door. She [the grandmother] has a rug pushed up against the door to prevent cold air from coming inside as the door does not meet the base of the frame tightly.

The blue walls have a few holes in them and the drapes are falling down. [Her] clothes hang on a clothesline which extends along the wall of her living room . . . A foul odor permeates the air . . . She sleeps in the den on a sofa.

When Singleton entered school, a psychologist found the youngster was functioning below average. Almost a decade later, Singleton, 15 at the time, was reading and doing arithmetic at the fifth-grade level.

Singleton was placed in special education classes at . . . elementary and . . . middle schools.

A [middle school] teacher described him as "desperate for friends but . . . has difficulty establishing relationships."

Schoolmates teased him about his unpleasant odor, caused by bedwetting.

To avoid the taunts, Singleton built a partition around his desk.

Early in [year], Singleton was convicted of burglary and theft and placed on probation.

While on probation, he violated curfew and exhibited behavior problems, and was placed in the Boys Attention Home, a house in Charlottesville for juveniles whose next step into the juvenile justice system would place them in a more restrictive state learning center.

His probation officer said that while Singleton was there he "refused to follow rules or complete chores and on several occasions left the program without permission."

He was transferred that summer to the Barrett Learning Center, a state juvenile detention facility in Hanover.

Authorities there initially noticed gradual improvement in Singleton's behavior. But eventually, he started cursing the staff and breaking the rules daily.

Source: McHugh (1987)

Questions About the Case
1. Should Tony's behavior have been disturbing to his community? Why or why not?
2. What would have been the advantages and disadvantages of early intervention in Tony's case? Where do you think Tony's behavior should have been addressed first, and why?
3. What is the best treatment or intervention for young people like Tony?

* * * *

It is not at all unusual for students with serious emotional or behavioral problems to carry a different label, particularly "learning disabled." Kate's teacher tells us about how students in her class said to have "learning disabilities" also had severe emotional and behavioral disorders (or severe "emotional disturbance" in the language of federal law). Again, as in the case of Tony, we see how life circumstances could contribute to an emotional or behavioral disorder. But we also see how difficult behavior can be episodic in school and how experiences at school can sometimes counterbalance conditions at home.

Kate

1 never thought I would see Kate Morrissey sitting with a group of girls and boys laughing and talking. The change in her had been remarkable. In a little more than a year, she had gone from a sullen, introverted, unpopular fifth grader to just another good kid.

Looking back, I remember thinking how confident I was starting the school year. I had been teaching for two years and still loved teaching despite the long hours it demanded. I had handled several difficult situations successfully since I left college; I was ready for anything—or so I thought. I looked at my roster of new students and wondered what surprises would be in store this year. In the first two years there had been challenges, but so far none that I couldn't handle. Had I known what was ahead, I probably would have taken a leave of absence. This class would require strength and energy I didn't even know I possessed.

It started with a note from the resource teacher telling me the names of the six students with learning disabilities who would be in my room. Our school had been using an inclusive model for resource help for several years now, so I knew I would have these students in my room most of the day. This didn't bother me because I had been successful in the past working with students who had both behavior and academic problems.

I decided to read the green files before meeting the students, so I could make preparations for their arrival. I made a list that included students' names and disabilities. Most of them were having difficulties with reading and math. A couple had behavior problems as well as academic problems, but still I thought I could handle these issues with help from the special education teacher. I must admit I did become concerned when I discovered that one of the students had severe emotional disturbance and had been violent in the past—punching a hole in the wall, breaking a window with his fist, and dislocating the principal's shoulder. It was definitely going to be an interesting year!

After school began I noticed there were many student issues I had not expected. Two students were identified for the gifted program, one student had been diagnosed with ADHD but was not on medication, one student had behavior problems stemming from sexual abuse, another student's mother was terminally ill, and then there was Kate. With everything else I had to do, how would I ever find the patience to deal with the tantrums, screaming, stubbornness, and the neediness of Kate? I knew teachers were supposed to be able to do it all, but this seemed overwhelming.

I had never run across a child like Kate. I knew from the moment I met her that she was incredibly bright. Unfortunately, her appearance and behavior put people off so quickly that most never took the time to get to know the "real" Kate. There may be more diplomatic ways to say it, but she was dirty, "smelled like a dog" (as a fellow student described her), and was totally unsociable. She always had her nose in a book—at lunch, at recess, and any time there was a break from structured activities in the classroom. I had to hand it to the other kids in class because they didn't tease; not much, anyway. Some of the children I had known through the years would have been unmerciful. Most of the students in the room ignored her. There was little interaction between Kate and the rest of the class.

It was obvious that Kate loved to read, but still I was somewhat surprised by Kate's score on the reading assessment: her instructional level was seventh grade. Her spelling inventory, however, showed she was a level-one speller. The disparity was stunning. Any kind of writing, even the unstructured variety in her journal, was extremely frustrating for her. Every Monday morning I had a battle with Kate when it was time for word study. The task was to use each word from the word list in a sentence. She hated to write. She would whine and mope, and often when I insisted she do the work, she became belligerent. She simply refused to write. The other children observed these episodes, of course, and sometimes they were frightened by Kate's actions. On more than one occasion, Kate screamed at me and pushed her book off the desk.

"OK, Kate, take your word study journal out of your desk and begin your sentences for this week," I said one morning. Kate just sat there staring defiantly at the floor. "Kate, it is time to start." Kate blurted, "I'm not going to do it, and you can't make me."

The mornings I could not cajole Kate into participating, I would give her a choice of going to time out in the room to do her work or going to the office. Once, when Kate chose not to work or go to time out, I called the office and asked the assistant principal to come to my room, which was actually a trailer outside the building. The assistant principal arrived and told Kate that she must go to the office to finish her work. Kate held on to her desk and would not move. I sensed that Kate was on the verge of an emotional explosion, so I had all of the other students line up to go to the library. Kate lined up too. As we walked to the library the assistant principal followed the group. When we passed by the office the assistant principal told Kate to go into the office, and Kate complied. I felt lucky that the strategy to get Kate to the office had worked without having a violent confrontation in our classroom.

Kate was puzzling. She could be so difficult. It was almost impossible to get her to do anything she didn't want to do. She would dig in her heels psychologically and simply refuse to cooperate. You could see her resistance in her posture. She folded her arms tight against her chest and looked off into space. What seemed totally incongruent and very surprising to me was Kate's sophisticated sense of humor. Early in the year she had begun to bring in cartoons from *The New Yorker* and show them to me. The two of us would howl as we read them. The other fifth-graders looked on in confusion, trying to understand what was so funny.

When I met Kate's mother and her mother's boyfriend at Back-to-School night, I didn't form much of an impression for good or ill. Her mother looked fairly plain. "Please tell me, Ms. Morrissey, do you work in the home or outside?" I asked. She replied, "I recently completed my master's degree in social work. I am a caseworker for the county social services department." Apparently she put in long hours, because she did not spend much time at home. "I'm glad to be finished with the long, frequent drives to night school. For several years I have been unable to spend much time with Kate in the evenings. I gave her so much independence in those days that she now resents it when I tell her what to do."

Ms. Morrissey's boyfriend was a little rough around the edges—short, chubby, a couple of days' growth of beard, and remarkably odoriferous. He wore a hunter's cap and his shirt and pants had the kind of gray cast that my family's clothes get when I use cheap detergent. What little he said was virtually inaudible, because he mumbled.

Ms. Morrissey asked some good questions about Kate. She expressed some concerns about her friendships, or lack of them. When I broached the topic of Kate's uncompleted homework assignments, Ms. Morrissey remarked, "That is Kate's responsibility. She knows what she is supposed to do. If I make suggestions she either acts as if I'm not there or refuses to do it." I also summoned up my courage to tell Ms. Morrissey about Kate's body odor. Her response was essentially the same: "That's her job too. She knows she is supposed to bathe every night. When I tell her to shower, she usually responds by throwing a tantrum that may last as long as half an hour."

Time might have passed with only minor rough spots in our classroom had 1 not decided to visit Kate's home. That visit set us up for what turned out to be a tense, troubling, and fairly long-lasting confrontation. It was in February after I had developed what I believed was a mutually caring relationship with Kate, even though I was beginning to discover that Kate was tight-lipped, even secretive, about her life outside of school.

I was becoming increasingly concerned because Kate had confided reluctantly that frequently nobody came home until 11:00 or 12:00 at night. Many nights, she was in the trailer all by herself, except for Sandy, her pet rat, and Rover, her beloved dog. She boasted that she could take care of herself and was not afraid, even though her trailer was in an isolated area. On these nights she fixed macaroni and cheese and treated herself with bags of Oreos. In fact, her reliance on sweets had begun to be apparent. She also told me about how messy things were at her house. She seemed quite pained to tell me these things. Kate would say things like, "You wouldn't believe what a mess my house is. You wouldn't want to come to my house."

When I looked back over my own journal, I realized that I had actually been building a case for making a home visit. Or, more accurately, my letters to myself seemed to compel me to visit Kate and her mother in their home. The opportunity for making a home visit fell into my lap when Kate sneaked her pet rat to school on the bus. Students are not allowed to have animals on the bus, so that evening I offered to give Kate a ride home and to take Sandy the Rat with us. In fear of what I might find, I invited the assistant principal to go with us.

When we arrived at the house, I discovered there was good reason to be concerned. The trailer was down a long, bumpy driveway, nowhere near any other houses. The trailer was old, the front steps sagged, and the storm door, hanging from its hinges, had a broken pane. The yard looked like the local junkyard and included an old refrigerator that had been used for target practice. But the worst was yet to come. Inside, half of the living room was piled from floor to ceiling with trash. A spot had been cleared on the couch just large enough for Kate to sit and watch TV. I could see how Kate might be overwhelmed by the enormity of the task of cleaning up the mess.

Kate had been assigned a Big Sister through a program at the university. Ms. Morrissey had told Kate that she couldn't see her Big Sister until the house had been cleaned. With the three of us working together—Kate, the assistant principal, and I—we figured we could at least take care of Kate's room. It didn't take long to discover that it wasn't possible. Her room was covered with trash, books were on the floor, all of her clothes were scattered around the room. Not one piece of clothing was in her closet. We started to pick up the trash, but soon stopped when I picked up a book and found dog feces on it. I looked down and realized I was standing in dog poop! Kate was right. The problem was just too big.

All of this happened on a Friday. I did not see her until the following Monday. When Kate arrived at school she was very angry with me. She gave me the cold shoulder. "Hi, Kate!" I said as she walked in the door and headed toward her desk. Kate did not respond.

I should have known not to press her, but she had made me angry too. She had been rude all morning. Once again, it was time to collect the sentences for word study. Kate would not hand in her notebook. I gave her an ultimatum and told her she must hand it in now. She looked at me and yelled, "This is my book. You can't have it. This is all your fault!" She threw the book at me, continued screaming, and started tipping over desks.

It took both the assistant principal and me to calm Kate. When she finally settled down, I was so emotionally exhausted that I could have walked out the door and never returned. Following the confrontation, the assistant principal and I agreed that what we needed was an all-out program to bring Kate into the mainstream of life in school, and somehow this effort had to include her mother. We had the will, and we hoped we had the energy, but what we didn't have was a strategy.

Source: Kauffman, Mostert, Trent, & Hallahan (2002, pp. 153–156)

Questions About the Case
1. Suppose that Kate's teacher had not made a home visit, how do you think she would have interpreted Kate's behavior differently?
2. Knowing the conditions in Kate's home, what do you think were the best strategies for Kate and her principal in dealing with Kate's mother?
3. What do you think would have been the best strategies for Kate's teacher to use in her classroom? The first paragraph of the case describes global changes in Kate's behavior in school. What do you think was likely responsible for these changes?

* * * *

Children and youth with emotional or behavioral disorders usually present problems to many of the people with whom they have contact. Most relevant here are the difficulties they cause teachers and peers at school. All veteran teachers of students with emotional or behavioral disorders recall incidents in which the pupils defeated their best efforts to instruct or maintain order. In many cases, teachers marvel at the wild antics of their students or the seemingly unsolvable puzzle their behavior presents. And in retrospect, many leading experts are amused by their own naïveté—which sometimes served them well and sometimes was disastrous—in dealing with students who are difficult to manage and teach.

Pearl Berkowitz

If you could look back and focus on my most vivid memory, you might see me, now the teacher in Mrs. Wright's former classroom, futilely hovering over two hyperactive 12-year-old girls who are fighting about which one should use the free half of an easel. On the other side of this easel, a big, burly, belligerent boy is calmly painting, secure in the knowledge that no one would dare question his right to do so. Standing near the window is a small, thin-faced, pale, remote-looking boy who is staring at the fish tank, apparently just watching the fish swim around. Next to him, another boy is sitting on the rocker tickling himself under the chin with the mink tails he has just cut off the collar of the school secretary's new spring coat. Two children, a boy and a girl, perched on the old dining table, are playing a loud game of checkers, while another boy is silently resting, stretched out atop an old upright piano that I had inveigled into my room. Sporadically, in the midst of this magnificent atmosphere for learning, some child says to another, "Your mother," and the entire class seems to leap together and land in a football pile-up on the floor while I stand helplessly by.

Of course I made many mistakes, but I hope I also learned something from each. Let me share just one of these early mistakes with you. I was doing my weekly planning when a brilliant idea occurred to me. I decided that the greatest contribution I could make that week would be to bring some culture into the lives of those poor, deprived, disturbed children at Bellevue. To start on this enriching experience, I elected to read to them a favorite poem from my own elementary school days, "The Owl and the Pussycat." Imagine my consternation at the chaos I caused when I reached the lines, "What a beautiful pussy you are, you are. What a beautiful pussy you are." The children actually tumbled out of my room with noisy screaming and guffawing. Within minutes, I was left alone in the classroom, bewildered and unaware of what had caused the difficulty. I had a lot to learn.

Source: Berkowitz (1974, pp. 30–31)

Questions About the Case

1. In what way(s) do you see Berkowitz's management of her class as typical of first-year teachers?

2. What are the strengths and weaknesses of Berkowitz's interactions with her students?

3. In what ways do you see specific children in Berkowitz's class as typical or atypical of children identified today as having EBD? How might EBD students be the same or different today compared to those in Berkowitz's class of the 1950s?

2. Cases on the Extent of Emotional and Behavioral Disorders

The following four brief cases should be considered together. For each, you are to consider whether the child or youth should be considered to have an emotional or behavioral disorder or not to be so classified. In many cases, there is disagreement among observers about whether a student should be identified for special education. You should be able to justify your decision about a particular child or youth.

Barry

Barry has five older siblings, the youngest of whom is 10 years older than he. He has always been the baby of the family in everyone's eyes, especially his mother's. He is now a rotund third grader whose torpor is remarkable. His obesity, sluggishness, and infantile behavior (e.g., he prefers to play with small stuffed animals) make him a constant and easy target for teasing by his classmates. Since he entered kindergarten, Barry's mother has brought him to school daily, sat in her car in the parking lot during the entire school day in case he should "need" her at any time, brought his lunch to him and fed him in the hall or in her car, and whisked him home after school. Her life seems absurdly devoted to his safety and comfort yet ironically calculated to impair his psychological and physical growth and development. School officials suspect that Barry was bottle-fed until he was in the second grade, and they know that his diet now consists primarily of junk foods. He has no friends his age, and he will not participate in age-appropriate play in the classroom or on the playground. He is constantly teased by other children because of his weight and infantile behavior.

Darlene

Darlene's mother was a 12-year-old sixth grader when Darlene was conceived. Recently graduated from high school, the mother is now pregnant with her third child. Darlene is a first grader who frequently gets into trouble because she hits or pokes other children, fails to do her work, and disobeys the teacher. Other children are beginning to shy away from her in fear. She is bright-eyed and gregarious with adults, and the casual observer may not suspect that the teacher sees her as a significant problem.

Nathan

Nathan is an eighth grader with an IQ in the gifted range. Although he is highly intelligent and creative and scores high on standardized achievement tests, his report cards contain only *D*s and *F*s. All his teachers and the school principal are exasperated with his constant clowning in class, his refusal to complete assignments (and his insistence that sloppy, incomplete work is sufficient), and his frequent macho behavior that gets him into fights with other students. His mother, a divorced former teacher, is at her wit's end with him at home; he is slovenly, refuses to do chores, threatens her and his older sister with physical violence, and was recently caught shoplifting.

Claudia

Claudia is the wispy 16-year-old daughter of a wealthy attorney. Her favorite book is the Bible; she is preoccupied with remaining slender in this life and earning the right to ecstatic happiness forever in the next. Her schoolwork is always perfect, or nearly so. She has only one close friend, a woman in her early 20s who has a history of suicide attempts. Claudia complains constantly of being tired, unable to sleep, and too fat. She is forever dieting and exercising, and she frequently vomits immediately after she eats a normal meal. She offers profuse apologies for any imperfection anyone points out in her behavior or academic performance.

Source: Personal experiences and accounts of other educators

Questions About the Cases
1. Which of these individuals (if any) do you think should be identified for special education as emotionally disturbed, and which (if any) do you think should not be? Why?
2. What kinds of behavior problems should be of greatest concern to teachers?
3. What should trigger identification of a child or youth as having mental health problems?
4. Should all mental health problems result in a student's being identified as needing special education? If so, why? If no, why not?

3. Cases on the History of Emotional and Behavioral Disorders and Current Issues

Perspectives on the behavior of children and youth change over time. However, such perspectives usually change rather slowly. Often we are not aware of how perspectives are changing in our own era. Some of the behavior that once was considered highly inappropriate or deviant is now considered unexceptional. Laws change. But community standards, which are really the basis for many laws, also change. You might consider how our ideas about misbehavior have changed in the past 150 years or so and how they have not changed much. You might also consider what change is desirable or undesirable in how we view children's behavior. Just because something changes doesn't mean is has changed for the better or for the worse. Some changes are good for our society and for children; some are not.

N. B.

N. B., aged 16, was described to me by his father, who came to consult with me in regard to his management, as a boy of singularly unruly and intractable character, selfish, wayward, violent without ground or motive, and liable under the paroxysm of his moodiness to do personal mischief to others; not, however, of a physically bold character. N.B. is of a fair understanding and exhibits considerable acuteness in sophisticated apologies for his wayward conduct. He has made little progress in any kind of study. His fancy is vivid, supplying him profusely with sarcastic imagery. He has been subjected at different times, and equally without effect, to a firmly mild and to a rigid discipline. In the course of these measures, solitary confinement has been tried but to this he was impassive. It produced no effect.

He was last in a very good [school] in a town in _____, where he drew a knife upon one of the officers of the establishment while admonishing him, and produced a deep feeling of aversion in the minds of his companions by the undisguised pleasure he showed at some bloodshed that took place in this town during the disturbance of 18__.

He has not appeared to be sensually disposed and he is careful of property. His

15

bodily health is good and he has never had any cerebral affection. This boy was further described to me as progressively becoming worse in his conduct and more savagely violent to his relatives. Still I easily discovered that he was unfavourably situated, for his relations appeared to be at once irritable and affectionate and the total failure of various plans of education was throwing him entirely upon their hands.

As an instance of the miserable pleasure which he took in exciting disgust and pain, I was told that when 13 years old, he stripped himself naked and exposed himself to his sisters.

Source: Mayo (1839, pp. 68–69)

Questions About the Case
1. What explanations can you offer for N. B.'s behavior?
2. What interventions are available today that were not in N. B.'s era?
3. How would N. B.'s behavior as described in this case be viewed today?

* * * *

We often do not perceive (or we forget) the personal experience of pain that someone with an emotional or behavioral disorder feels. Sheldon Rappaport, a leading figure in the field of learning disabilities, describes some of his painful school-related experiences as a child. His experiences are much like those of many children with emotional or behavioral disorders.

Sheldon R. Rappaport

That school day had been like all others—bright with the joy of being with children and blurred in a kaleidoscope of activity. But in late afternoon, there was something different in the way Miss Joseph asked us to take our seats. Her customary calm and warmth were missing. On top of that, she announced that the principal had come to talk to us. My stomach squinched "danger."

The principal, small, grayed, and austere, spoke in her usually clipped fashion

16

about the importance of working hard in school. As her train of thought thundered by, I was aware only of its ominous roar. The meaning of her words did not come into focus until she made the pronouncement: "Those boys and girls who have frittered away their time, and as a consequence will not be promoted to second grade, will stand when I call their names." Then she called my name.

The shock and mortification staggered me, making it difficult to struggle out of my seat and stand beside my desk. Who stood when she called the other names, the faces of those who remained seated, and what further remarks she intoned all blurred into a macabre dance that encircled my shame. Breathing was painful and had, I was sure, a ridiculously loud rasp which was heard by everyone. My legs rebelled at supporting my weight, so my fingers, aching tripods of ice, shared the burden. In contrast to the cold of my numbed face were the hot tears that welled in my eyes and threatened to spill down my cheeks to complete my degradation.

The principal left. Class was over. Amid joyous shouts, children milled through the door that for them was the entrance to summer fun and freedom. Some may have spoken to me, to tease or to console, but I could not hear them. The warm and pretty Miss Joseph was there, speaking to me, but I could neither hear nor respond. The borders of my mind had constricted like a hand clutching my pain.

Daily I sat staring at a book that would not surrender to me its meaning. In my war with the book, now and again I was victorious over an isolated word, but the endless legion of pages ultimately defeated me. Repeatedly, I looked back over the unfriendly, unyielding rows of print to find a word that I could recognize. In doing so, my failures amassed by the minute, like a swelling mob jeering at me. Finally, the fury rising within me burst from my fists, while from between clenched teeth I silently cursed the head I was pounding. To me, the immutable reality was that my head was bad. It caused my frustration. It sponsored my shame. I knew no alternative but to beat it into becoming a smarter head. That failed, too, adding daily to my feelings of frustration and worthlessness.

Daily terrors were walking the eight blocks to and from school and going into the school yard for recess. Being all flab and clumsiness and wearing thick glasses made me a ready target for any kid who needed to prove his prowess by beating me up. And the number who needed that were legion. Consequently, a rainy day became a reprieve. To awaken to a rainy morning was like an eleventh-hour stay of execution. It meant no recess outdoors. And nobody who wanted to fight. But even better than a rainy morning was being ill. Only then, in my bed, in my room, did I feel really secure. In the fall of third grade I missed twenty-two days of school. I was confined to bed with rheumatic fever, as I learned from the family doctor when I didn't have the desired wind for distance running while in college. Despite pains which I can still vividly recall, that confinement is the most peaceful of all my childhood memories.

The only outdoor activities I enjoyed were pretend ones. (The woman who lived in the next row house must have been sainted.) To get me out of the house, my mother put on the open porch the piano stool I played with. It became the steering wheel of a huge, powerful truck (you know how loud they are), which I guided flawlessly along endless highways, gaining the admiration of all whom I passed. At other times, I ventured across the street where the vacant lot became a battlefield on which I, clothed in my father's army tunic and overseas cap, performed feats of heroism and distinction for which I received countless medals and accolades. Those fantasized moments of glory apparently nourished my thin strand of self-respect enough to enable it to withstand the daily siege on my pride.

At night, when the cannonade of derision was still and my imperiled pride temporarily safe, I implored God and the Christ, Jesus, to see to it that tomorrow would not hold for me the tortures of today. I offered all possible concessions and deals, but relentlessly the tomorrows of Monday to Friday were no better.

Source: Rappaport (1976, pp. 347–350)

Questions About the Case
1. Could Rappaport's experiences be very similar to those of a student in public schools today? Why or why not?
2. How might school experiences like Rappaport's be affected by today's emphasis on student achievement, test performance, and accountability?
3. Given a student and terrors like Rappaport's self-description, how can teachers best handle bullying behavior on the part of other students?

4. Cases on Conceptual Models of Emotional and Behavioral Disorders

A biogenic model makes physiological processes the center of attention. However, it does not rule out all other types of intervention. The assumption is that the youngster's difficulties are of neurological origin and can be treated effectively, at least to some extent, by medications.

Elizabeth

Elizabeth was diagnosed with schizophrenia as a young child. She is now a tenth grader and her illness has been in remission for two years. However, she has gone through years of struggle with a variety of emotional and behavioral disorders for which medications were prescribed. In elementary school, her academic performance deteriorated markedly between first and third grade, and she had trouble getting along with other children. She also had difficulty paying attention and completing her school work.

The first psychiatrist who treated Elizabeth thought she had attention deficit disorder because of her difficulty in paying attention, completing tasks, and getting along with other children. Consequently, the psychiatrist prescribed Ritalin for Elizabeth. Her performance improved considerably early in the fourth grade when she was taking Ritalin. However, within a few months it became apparent that Elizabeth was suffering from another disorder.

When psychiatrists discovered that Elizabeth was having auditory hallucinations and sometimes visual hallucinations accompanying the voices she heard, she was hospitalized. Because she had terrible headaches along with the hallucinations, imaging techniques were used to check her brain for tumors or other neurological problems that could cause her symptoms. Nothing was found wrong with her brain. Consequently, the psychiatrist's decision was to place Elizabeth on a neuroleptic (antipsychotic) drug, a major tranquilizer called Mellaril. This drug kept the effects of her illness under enough control so that Elizabeth could go home and return to school. Although Mellaril has been very helpful, her support from her family and teachers has also been very important in allowing her to function well in school and at home.

Source: Anonymous (1994)

Questions About the Case
1. What reasons can you give for viewing schizophrenia as a mental illness of biological origin rather than as an emotional or behavioral disorder with causes in life circumstances?
2. What early symptoms of mental illness did Elizabeth exhibit, and why might treatment of them with medication be wise?
3. Besides medication, what other interventions do you think would have been important in Elizabeth's case?

* * * *

The psychoeducational model attempts to combine concern for functioning in the present with understanding of underlying motivations for behavior. Although other conceptual models do not discount the importance of talking to students, the psychoeducational model sees talking with the student about behavior as the primary strategy.

Aaron

Fourteen-year-old Aaron was referred for special education because of his oppositional and sometimes verbally threatening behavior. In addition to being noncompliant with adults' instructions, he frequently leaves the classroom without permission and roams the hallways. He appears to enjoy confrontations with teachers and taunts his peers, especially a deaf student in the class, Drew, who also has minimal social skills. The type of intervention his teacher uses is illustrated by the way she handled a particular incident.

One morning, Drew came to school very agitated, requiring the teacher to spend most of her time before lunch calming him down. At lunch, Aaron persistently aggravated Drew. When the teacher told Aaron to stop and return to his desk, Aaron began yelling that Drew had called him a "fag" and that he, Drew, was the one who should return to his desk. When the teacher repeated her instruction, Aaron shoved a desk across the room and left the classroom without permission.

Pacing the hall, he began disturbing other students. The teacher and another staff member then escorted Aaron to a quiet room, to which he went without resistance. In the quiet room, the teacher used LSI techniques to help Aaron think through the reasons for his behavior and how he might behave in more adaptive ways.

Through skillful interviewing about the incident with Drew, the teacher was able to help Aaron see that he is jealous and resentful of the time she spends with Drew. Aaron lives with his mother and an older sister who has multiple disabilities, is very low functioning, and demands a lot of his mother's attention. His father left home when Aaron was eight years old, and his mother is not in good health. This means that Aaron has had to take on some adult responsibilities at an early age. The goals of the teacher's LSI about this particular incident were to get Aaron to understand that she cares about him, that she wants to prevent him from disrupting the group, and, most important, that there are similarities in his situation at home and at school that give rise to similar feelings and behavior.

Aaron's teacher used what James and Long (1992) have called a "Red Flag Interview," a discussion that addresses the problem of transferring problems from home to school. A Red Flag Interview follows a predictable sequence in which a student such as Aaron is helped to understand that (1) he experiences a stressful situation at home (e.g., a beating, overstimulation, etc.); (2) his experience triggers intense feelings of anger, helplessness, and so on; (3) these feelings are not expressed to the abusive person at home because he is fearful of retaliation; (4) he contains his feelings until he is getting on the bus, entering the school, or responding to a demand; and (5) he acts out his feelings in an environment that is safer and directs his behavior toward someone else.

Although the LSI may be based on psychoanalytic notions of defense mechanisms, it also must end with a return to the reality of the situation. In Aaron's situation, this meant his return to the class and anticipation of future problems. His teacher ended the LSI as follows:

> *Interviewer:* "What do you think Drew might do when we walk into the room?"

Aaron: "He will probably point at me and laugh."

Interviewer: "That might happen. How can you deal with that?"

Aaron: "I can ignore him."

Interviewer: "That will not be easy for you. It will take a lot of emotional strength to control your urge to tease him back. And if you do that and Drew teases you, who is going to get into trouble?"

Aaron: "Drew."

Interviewer: "That's right. You are now beginning to think more clearly about your actions. Also, I will set up a behavior contract for you. If you are able to ignore Drew's teasing, you will earn positive one-on-one time with me."

Aaron: "Agreed."

Source: James & Long (1992, p. 37)

Questions About the Case
1. If Aaron's maladaptive behavior persists, what options should the teacher consider?
2. In what way(s) did the interview of Aaron connect underlying motivations, present problems, and future problems?
3. In what way(s) did the interviewer use techniques associated with other conceptual models?

＊ ＊ ＊ ＊

An ecological model focuses on the social context of a student's behavior. The student is seen as part of a social system that can be changed to support desirable behavior. Emelda's case demonstrates how the study of multiple, naturally occurring variables in a classroom environment can reveal which ones are most effective in controlling a student's progress. An ecological approach may encompass multiple variables in a classroom. It could also involve multiple variables in the school, community, family, or a combination of these.

Emelda

Emelda, a 10-year-old with autism, attended a special self-contained class in a public school. She spoke in complete sentences but exhibited echolalia—parroting words, phrases, or sentences she heard. Academically, she was performing at about second-grade level. The primary objective of intervention was to increase her rate of correct academic responding. The first step was to observe the naturally occurring ecological, teacher, and student variables in the class. Ecological variables included such things as the particular activity (e.g., language), tasks being presented (e.g., discussion, use of media), physical arrangement (e.g., class divided into groups), and instructional grouping (e.g., one-to-one or small group). Teacher variables included who (teacher or aide) was giving instruction, whether the teacher was at the desk or among the students, and various categories of the teacher's behavior (e.g., whether demanding an academic response, focusing on one student, giving approval or disapproval). Student variables were such things as whether Emelda was participating in the task, moving about the classroom, paying attention, or engaging in off-task behavior such as self-stimulation.

Through correlation of ecological, teacher, and student variables with Emelda's correct responses to academic tasks, teachers and researchers found the naturally occurring procedures that were most effective in helping her learn. The conditions under which Emelda and other students learned most effectively included the following:

- 3 to 5 students per group
- combinations of verbal interaction (discussion formats) with media (e.g., pictures or drawings of what is being discussed)
- individualized sets of media materials for each student
- 5-minute rotations of media/concept presentations
- a minimum of three sets of materials to teach each concept

- frequent group (choral) responding
- fast-paced *random* responding (i.e., not calling on students in a predictable order)
- serial responding—3 to 5 quick responses per student
- frequent student-to-student interactions

Source: Kamps et al. (1991, p. 377)

Questions About the Case

1. What are the aspects of Emelda's social system or context that needed to be altered?
2. How is the ecological approach compatible with a behavioral model?
3. Supposing that altering the social context does little or nothing to change a student's behavior (remember that *nothing always works*), what alternatives would you suggest, and why?

* * * *

The behavioral model focuses on problem behavior and ways to influence it. The basic idea is to use manipulation of the environment, especially what happens just before and what happens just after behavior, to change the way a student behaves.

Sven

Sven was an 11-year-old attending a special self-contained class for students with emotional or behavioral disorders. His teacher described him as showing inadequate attention to tasks, inappropriate and aggressive talk, and physically aggressive behavior. An observer recorded Sven's behavior during brief (15-second) intervals for 15 to 30 minutes of his English lesson each day. These observations showed that he was engaged in academic tasks less than 60 percent of the time on average and that his behavior was disruptive about 40 percent of the time.

Those working with Sven assumed that students who exhibit maladaptive

24

behavior may do so for a variety of reasons, including not only the consequences of behavior but the setting in which it occurs and the demands for performance: the antecedents. In this case, antecedents related to Sven's maladaptive behavior were changed. The antecedents of his off-task, disruptive behavior—what he was assigned to do, especially if it was an assignment he did not like—seemed to be at least as much a problem as the consequences of his behavior. Therefore, the primary strategy used to modify Sven's behavior was to give him his choice of six to eight task options in his English class. The task options were constructed as variations on the work he normally would do, any one of which was acceptable and would lead to the same instructional objective. Under these conditions, Sven engaged in academic tasks about 95 percent of the time, and his disruptive behavior dropped to an average of about 10 percent.

Clearly, giving Sven choices about his assignments—all of the choices being acceptable variations—improved his attention to his tasks and decreased his disruptive behavior markedly. Although rewarding consequences for appropriate behavior and academic performance are critically important, teachers may also use knowledge of behavior principles to alter the conditions of instruction in ways that defuse task resistance and encourage task attention.

Source: Dunlap et al. (1994)

Questions About the Case
1. Usually, we think of the behavioral approach as emphasizing consequences—rewards for desired behavior, for the most part. What behavior principles does the case of Sven illustrate?
2. How does the case of Sven emphasize the importance of a teacher's relating to the student as a thinking and feeling person, even if the behavioral model is being implemented?
3. What are all the factors that, according to a behavioral approach, influence behavior?

5. Cases on Evaluation for Identification of Emotional and Behavioral Disorders

Prereferral interventions sometimes solve problems and avoid referral to special education. Consider the case of Amy, for whom referral was averted.

Amy

Characteristics: Amy was a fifth-grade student more than 2 years behind academically, with Chapter I remedial assistance in reading and math. Family stressors included a blended family (stepfather, stepsisters), alcoholic grandmother, and a disorganized home life, but family members were loving toward the child. Two instances of sexual molestation by an acquaintance had been reported.

Behaviors: Student self-reported feelings of unworthiness; explosive behaviors occurred when corrected. She also exhibited unpredictable mood swings, made loud and irrelevant comments, and stole from and displayed aggression toward peers. The student reported people were following her and that she could hear negative thoughts of others.

Monitoring system: Amy requested earning points; thus, a point sheet was designed for academics (i.e., begin work, ask for help when needed, work without disturbing others) and behaviors (i.e., follow directions, accept correction, keep hands to self). The student self-recorded warnings or reminders, with a review every hour by the teacher and a tally at the end of each day with the school nurse. Points earned activities with selected persons.

Follow-up/maintenance: Eventually, the student was able to control her behaviors, with less-frequent reporting to the teacher. In addition, a social skills and problem-solving group including other fifth-grade girls was conducted twice per week to assist in maintaining positive peer interactions.

Source: Noll, Kamps, & Seaborn (1993, p. 209)

Questions About the Case
1. Amy's problems were handled with prereferral, which was implemented only after she had considerable difficulty in school. Could they have been, or should they have been addressed earlier, and, if so, how?
2. What agencies other than the school should have been involved in Amy's case?
3. What should Amy's teacher have done had other agencies not become involved in the case?

* * * *

Nearly all professionals agree that a referral is not justified just because a teacher observes that a student misbehaves or has an academic problem in the classroom. Nevertheless, professionals often disagree about how much effort to expend on accommodating the student's needs before the teacher requests an evaluation for special education. School systems are increasingly likely to require teachers to complete referral forms on which they describe behavioral characteristics and prereferral strategies. Consider the following two cases of Don and Bill, and imagine that you had to make decisions based solely on the information provided here.

Don

Don is a second grader whose teacher provides the following reasons for referral. "His behavior is continually disruptive. He is verbally abusive and physically aggressive. He will not follow instructions (such as to get proper book out, put candy away, ask for permission to leave the room, etc.). He uses vulgar, offensive words. He is untruthful." The teacher judges his academic performance to be average in spelling, handwriting, social studies, and physical education; below average (but not failing) in reading, language, arithmetic, science, and music. No recent test scores are reported.

Don's mother was contacted about a month ago, when she was asked to come to school following Don's suspension. She is aware of Don's behavior problems and is cooperative with school personnel. She is aware of Don's referral and is in agreement with it.

Don was retained in first grade. He has so far attended three different schools. His current teacher reports that she contacted Don's previous teachers, who reported similar problems but had no suggestions for his management. The resource teacher has suggested and tried several different behavior management strategies, none of which has been successful. Don's current teacher has tried behavioral contracting, preferential seating, and peer tutoring, as well as reasoning with him, trying to help him see the consequences of unacceptable behavior, isolating him from peers, withholding all or part of his recess, sending him to the principal, and changing his placement to a classroom with fewer troublesome students. These strategies have been tried for a period of about two months; none has been successful.

Source: Contributed by Betty Hallenbeck

Bill

Bill is a 14-year-old eighth grader with a history of fighting, defiance, disruption, and lewd conduct. His present placement is in a special education resource room, with participation in as many regular classes as possible. School staff, including a behavioral consultant, have been devising special behavior management plans for him during the past year. He is now being referred for possible placement in a more restrictive residential setting.

At the beginning of the school year, Bill was harassing certain female staff members. This was dealt with by teaching Bill alternatives to staring (such as glancing) and by informing him of the severe consequences that would result from his staring, making slurping noises, and vocalizing or mouthing lewd remarks. He has responded well to this program and has been penalized only once for lewd behavior.

The program in effect at the beginning of the school year included a general behavior checklist on which Bill's behavior was rated each period on each of five behaviors: followed directions, participated, paid attention, completed classwork, and turned in homework. Teachers rated each behavior on the following scale: 3 = Great!, 2 = OK, 1 = Not acceptable, ? = Not applicable. Points could be earned for scoring threes and lost for scoring ones. Earned points could be exchanged in homeroom and during seventh period for activities and free time. Instruction in desirable classroom behavior was provided in homeroom. This plan was in effect from the beginning of school through mid-October. Bill could exhibit the desired behaviors, but he performed them sporadically.

In mid-October a set of consequences for resource and regular class settings was added for Bill's disruptive behavior. Regular classroom teachers were given the option of a quick ejection from their class (ignore, warn, eject); resource teachers were given the option of keeping him after school and having him walk home.

Because Bill was ending up in the office too much to suit the principal, even with the added consequences, additional interventions were tried. Direct observations were made to determine the extent to which Bill was following directions, including obeying classroom rules. He was found to be compliant with directions and rules about 60 to 75 percent of the time on average; he was engaging in a high level of disruptive and defiant behavior, and his compliance tended to fluctuate wildly (for example, from 0 to 86 percent compliance on one day). More explicit systems of penalties and rewards were devised; a "levels" plan was implemented, in which Bill could earn greater freedom and independence in school, plus food rewards, for improved behavior. Bill earned edible rewards on two occasions and then stated that he was no longer interested in "behaving for burgers."

In addition to the contingencies devised for Bill, the behavioral consultant has been providing instruction in social skills. These skills include asking for help from staff and responding appropriately to confusing and/or contradictory instructions or queries from staff.

Bill's behavior has been extremely variable from day to day since the beginning of school. Although he has reached several specific goals (e.g., not being ejected from more than 4 classes in 10 days), there has been no general trend toward improvement. In fact, Bill was recently suspended from school for one day.

Source: Contributed by Lee Jones

Questions About the Cases
1. Are the referrals justifiable in either or both of these cases? If so, why? If not, what additional information or level of detail or specificity would make them

justifiable?

2. What prereferral interventions, if any, do you think should have been employed in these two cases?

3. To what extent and in what ways did the teachers in these two cases do what they should have *before* referral?

6. Cases on Evaluation for Teaching Students with Emotional and Behavioral Disorders

Ray's case illustrates the point that evaluation may need to involve assessment of more than just the student's problem behavior. The reasonable explanation for Ray's behavior was not immediately obvious, and it is often the case that family factors in apparent emotional or behavioral problems are difficult to ferret out. Appropriate intervention in this case would have focused on resolving the abuse of Ray's mother as well as increasing his school attendance.

Ray

Throughout elementary school, Ray's teachers described him as a bright, cooperative, and sociable student. His work habits and general attitude toward school were very good. He achieved at or above grade level in all subjects and was popular among his peers. During the first few months of junior high school, all of Ray's teachers gave a similar general description. By the middle of seventh grade, however, Ray's behavior had changed dramatically.

Ray was absent from school with increasing frequency. He dropped out of all the extracurricular activities in which he had formerly participated. His teachers reported that he did not often complete assignments, frequently daydreamed in class, and was generally uninvolved in class activities. His grades dropped below passing.

Ray's teachers attempted to alter his behavior by a variety of means. They gave verbal praise, additional privileges, and points exchangeable for tangible rewards contingent upon appropriate behavior, but these techniques did not produce the desired behavior changes. Curricular modifications were made repeatedly, but Ray remained uninvolved in classroom activities. In fact, he was absent from school more and more frequently as time went on. He was unwilling to discuss the problem with his teachers or the guidance counselor. Phone calls and letters to his parents went unanswered. Only after being warned of a potential fine for truancy did Ray's parents agree to discuss the situation with school personnel. A conference was arranged with Ray, his parents, his teachers, and the guidance counselor.

31

During the conference, Ray's parents stated that he remained at home during his absences from school. The relationship between Ray and his mother appeared to be overly solicitous (they greeted each other with a kiss and held hands during most of the discussion). Ray's father was attentive but generally silent throughout the conference. Both parents agreed to make certain that Ray would attend school regularly.

Over the next few weeks, Ray's attendance improved only slightly. The case was then referred to the school mental health team, which was comprised of the teachers, a guidance counselor, a social worker, the school psychologist, and a psychiatrist. Reviewing the case, the psychiatrist emphasized that Ray had unmet dependency needs and was experiencing separation anxiety. The teachers initiated activities the psychiatrist recommended to enhance Ray's self-concept, increase his independence, and develop his sense of autonomy and control. Demonstrable results, in terms of improved attendance rates, were not evident after a month of such efforts.

As the final effort before taking legal action against Ray's parents, the social worker made a home visit one day when Ray was absent. Upon her arrival, the social worker found Ray comforting his obviously battered mother. His mother then revealed that her husband, an alcoholic, had been fired from his job a few months earlier. During this period of unemployment, he frequently drank excessively and became physically abusive toward her. When Ray was home, however, his father was usually not abusive or beat Ray's mother less severely.

Source: Contributed by James Krouse

Questions About the Case

1. How can teachers be aware of students' problems at home, and what can they do about such problems?
2. If you were responsible for Ray's education, what would be your primary objectives?
3. What kinds of things should prompt you to assess problems other than a student's behavior in your class?

Sometimes there seems to be no perceptible adversity in the life of a youngster with emotional or behavioral disorders. Then we wonder why the youngster is acting so awful, because we observe that he or she appears to have many advantages and little or nothing to complain about. If we try to put ourselves in the shoes of the student, we think we'd be very happy and behave ourselves. Sometimes on closer inspection we find that outward appearances (e.g., family affluence) are deceiving, that the youngster is really experiencing difficult circumstances that are generally well hidden. But that is not always the case. Sometimes we cannot find an apparent reason for the problem in the youngster's life circumstances.

Mark

The nervous, anxious, and seemingly hostile adolescent sat on the far side of the 6-foot classroom table. He fingered a pack of Marlboros, turning them over and over. His concentration was intense, unrelenting, compulsive, almost as if he hoped, by concentrating on the cigarettes, to direct the thoughts of the alternative school's staff away from him.

At first glance, he looked more like a candidate for admission to one of the better prep schools than for a slot in an alternative program. He was wearing a blue oxford-cloth shirt, cream-colored cords, and docksiders. He hadn't bothered to tuck the shirt in and one button too many had been left open . . .

He arrived at school early enough on the first day to claim the coveted last desk in the last row. He systematically walled in his space. The back of his chair was always against the classroom wall. Books, papers, pencils, pens; anything he owned was strewn, like a fortress, on the floor around his desk . . .

Mark was maniacal about keeping his space for himself. He wanted no one near him and would become verbally abusive if anyone touched him. He was struggling for attention, and at the same time refusing to accept it.

Mark's verbal contortions ranged from sophisticated wit to murderous descriptions of the ways he would eliminate his prime adversary in the classroom (me) to new and unheard of vulgarities.

When a very slow student in the class was awed on learning that Mark lived in the best section of town, he explained that the only difference was that [sparkling water] came out of the Matthews' faucets.

At least once a day he would consider himself victimized, and me the victimizer. Requests for classwork were considered irrational. Requests for a halt to a variety of obscenities were considered unfounded. Any request that required some form of cooperation was considered untimely. After refusing to participate, Mark would offer vivid details on his latest plan for my elimination. These would often come after I would reach out to him and especially after I would try to touch him.

Mark created many new vulgarities and embellished old ones with disarmingly picturesque terms. The adults associated with the program were well over 30 and none of us had heard many of Mark's vulgarities. One staff member began compiling a working dictionary of Mark's barbarisms . . .

He was often sent to the solitary confinement of "the cubicle" to stop his disruption of the class and permit other students to work. I spent hours there with him looking at and talking to the hurt, intelligent eyes of a superior being. Repeatedly, he rejected verbal or physical contact.

As the school year drew to a close, his nervous, compulsive, repetitive behavior intensified. Even while sitting still, he seemed to be pacing the walls in the parameters of his being. His concentrated mental isometrics were increasingly painful, trying, and irrational.

Source: Maruskin-Mott (1986, p. 53)

Questions About the Case
1. Supposing that you were to conduct a functional behavioral assessment (FBA) in this case, exactly what would you do?
2. If you were Mark's teacher, how would you have planned for his instruction?
3. Supposing that you were to devise a positive behavioral intervention plan for Mark, how would you go about it? What behavior would you encourage, support, or reinforce, and how would you do it?

7. Cases on Biological Factors in Emotional and Behavioral Disorders

Sometimes the biological basis of deviant behavior seems clear. Even so, there may be disagreement about the extent to which a youngster (or adult, for that matter) is cognizant of his or her inappropriate behavior and should be held responsible for his or her actions.

Chad

Chad's mother suspected that her son had schizophrenia long before psychiatrists diagnosed him as having the mental disorder. He had always been somewhat odd, engaging in head-banging as an infant in his crib and, when he was older, rubbing his head on the grass until he was bleeding. He also had some ritualistic behavior, such as knocking on a chair before he could sit down. As a child, he repeated over and over before going to sleep, "I'm not going to die, I'm not going to die…" His mother eventually became terrified that Chad would kill himself.

Chad was a bright student with a high grade point average in elementary school. But he was the classic high school "nerd" who didn't date or play sports. Before going to college, he'd earned enough money from selling computers he'd built from parts he bought online to buy a car. In college, he majored in business and computer science.

However, all did not go well in college. He managed to stay at college only one year. First, he was arrested for drunk and disorderly conduct and possession of marijuana, something totally out of character with his upbringing and prior behavior. But his parents were unaware that he'd become psychotic, not just fallen in with bad friends. He became convinced that his scrotum was abnormally large, although a doctor told him that there was nothing physically wrong. He became convinced that his scrotum was so big that it tipped his pelvis forward, making his back rigid and his head tip back. And he felt that people could tell this, that they were calling him "nerd" and "faggot" behind his back. His friends told him they thought he was crazy.

In April of his freshman year, Chad did tell his father by email that he was getting paranoid. He also imagined that his eyes were always glassy white and that he

35

could see a lot of blood vessels in his eyes. His parents thought he was having an anxiety attack. But he stopped going to classes and ended up with an F, 3 Ds and a C for his course grades.

When his parents picked him up from college in early May, after classes had ended, Chad was uncommunicative. At home, he stayed in his room nearly all the time, seldom bathed, slept all day, and spent the night on his computer. His mother heard him saying such things as "Shut up!" but he denied he was doing anything other than "messing with" her.

Ten days after coming home from college, Chad told his mother about his scrotum. He started cutting holes in his underwear, taping his scrotum up, and wearing the tightest jock strap he could find. His mother took him to the family doctor, who assured Chad that there was nothing wrong with his scrotum. He wasn't convinced, so his mother took him to a urologist, who told Chad the same thing. Chad did not believe the urologist, either.

Thinking that Chad might be schizophrenic, his mother took him to a psychiatrist, who suggested that Chad had "symptoms of a delusional nature and depressive obsessions" and prescribed Prozac and Zyprexa. However, Chad showed minimal improvement with these drugs, which he did not always take, and he started hallucinating (e.g., yelling at nonexistent "oystermen" to shut up because they were yelling at him). He told his mother that he'd found a plastic surgeon online who would do the necessary operation on him for $4000.

Chad wondered how he could get the money. He tried printing fake money with his computer, but he threw it away because it looked too phony. Before he robbed the bank, Chad tried to perform the surgery on himself. He stopped because of the blood and the pain. Robbing the bank seemed to him the only way to get the money for the surgery. He wore a black knit cap with eye holes cut in it and put on black gloves. He had no weapon of any kind, but he yelled "Put your hands up, this is a hold up!" when he entered the bank about 20 miles from his home.

Now he is in jail and could face life in prison. The local prosecutor has charged him not only with bank robbery but also with counterfeiting (remember, Chad had printed bills with his computer, which even the prosecutor admits were too crude to fool most people). The prosecutor maintains that although Chad is mentally ill, he knew that what he was doing was wrong. And if a defendant can tell right from wrong, then he should be prosecuted to the full extent of the law.

Source: Carlson (2003)

Questions About the Case
1. How is Chad's behavior consistent with the onset of schizophrenia in childhood and adolescence?
2. How do you think schools could have responded better to Chad's problems?
3. To what extent do you believe Chad should be held responsible for his behavior? Why?

* * * *

Biological factors are known to contribute significantly to schizophrenia. However, there are biological factors in all types of emotional and behavioral disorders, including depression.

Peter

Peter is 14 and was referred by his pediatrician due to nonspecific somatic (bodily) complaints, lethargy, psychomotor retardation, substantial weight gain, and frequent napping following his father's murder. Peter had been close to his father, and his interpersonal and academic functioning declined precipitously following his father's death. He spent hours alone in his room saying that he wished he were dead. He said he was too sad to cry. His family was afraid for his safety. His mother and older brother had been taking antidepressants since Peter's father's death, and both reported that the medication was helpful. The family had a history of depression, alcohol abuse, and anxiety. Given the severity of Peter's symptoms, his thinking of suicide, and other family members' positive response to antidepressants, Peter was started on antidepressant medication as well as cognitive-behavioral therapy.

Source: Kaslow, Morris, & Rehm (1998)

Questions About the Case
1. What biological risk factors are evident in this case?
2. What reasons would you have for suggesting that Peter's problems were reactive to the circumstance, not biological in origin?
3. If you were Peter's teacher, what could you do to help address his problems most effectively?

8. Cases on Family Factors in Emotional and Behavioral Disorders

Sometimes we can see risk factors at work in a child's home environment. Problem behavior seems to be passed from one generation to the next, not merely through genetic predispositions or other biological factors such as poor prenatal care but through the deviant behavior of parents. We are tempted to overgeneralize and assume that all misbehavior is a fault of parenting. Sometimes it appears to be, but sometimes it is decidedly not.

Sylvain

Sylvain lives with his mother and older sister. Welfare is his mother's only income. His mother has suffered from depression since age 16, was identified by her peers as both highly aggressive and socially withdrawn in the fourth grade, did poorly in school but finished high school, and is separated from her husband, who was drug dependent and physically abusive.

Sylvain' mother had anemia and diabetes when she was pregnant with him and had to take medication to stop contractions beginning in the seventh month of her pregnancy. Sylvain was born prematurely, and his umbilical cord was wrapped around his neck. At the age of 4 months, he was diagnosed with asthma. He also has chronic otitis (ear infections) and diarrhea. He has been on medication for hyperactivity since he was a year old. He has temper tantrums, is aggressive, and has a tendency to hurt himself. His mother feels inadequate in dealing with these problems.

Source: Serbin et al. (2002)

Questions About the Case
1. What parent and family factors put Sylvain at risk for the development of serious emotional and behavioral disorders?
2. How would you assess the relative contributions of biological and psychological factors in Sylvain's problems?
3. What supports do you think Sylvain's mother needs if she is to deal with his problems most productively?

Sometimes it is easy to miss problems. We make unwarranted assumptions or are unaware of important information. Sometimes we focus so much on school that we miss what's important outside of the school environment. Jack is a case in point.

Jack

I have been a teacher for over 10 years, beginning my career as a preschool teacher, then a first grade regular classroom teacher, and then a high school special education teacher for students with learning disabilities and emotional/behavioral disorders. Over the years I have encountered a number of students, too many really, whose lives have tugged at my heart-strings. After more than 10 years of working with kids, I believed that I had seen or at least heard just about everything. Then came Jack.

At the time of his referral, Jack was 15 years old, repeating the ninth grade, and receiving failing grades in most of his classes. The referring teacher said that Jack regularly entered her class in "crisis mode," pacing back and forth in clear distress. Many times, she wrote, this was in response to his younger brother, Drew, who was receiving special education services as a student with a learning disability. Drew was frequently removed from his 4th period special education class because of inappropriate behaviors and placed in the hallway near Jack's classroom. Jack would then feel compelled to talk with Drew in an effort to keep him from getting into more trouble. Jack would mutter, "there is going to be trouble" if he was not allowed to calm Drew down.

In addition to worrying about Drew, the teacher wrote, Jack also frequently placed himself in the middle of other students' problems and had difficulty leaving the stress of these situations outside of the classroom. Every day when he arrived in class, he asked to go see his guidance counselor or to attend mediation or to go to the attendance office or to go see one student or another because so-and-so was gossiping about someone else. She indicated that Jack had not had any major outbursts in class, but if his requests were not granted immediately he would become frantic and begin cursing to himself.

The referring teacher also described her various attempts at resolving Jack's problems. In an effort to redirect his anger or alleviate his worry, she reported, she would converse with Jack in the hallway nearly every time he came to class. She reported that he was fairly responsive to this "positive attention" but it would only "work" temporarily, as he would usually feel the need to stay in the hallway a little longer or go to guidance following these talks.

The teacher reported that she and the collaborative special education teacher, who was also in the classroom, would allow Jack a little more freedom of movement than the other students in the class. She stated that for the benefit of the rest of the class if Jack chose to disengage from the lesson by lying on the sofa and feigning sleep, then the teachers would respect his choice.

The referring teacher also wrote she had talked extensively with Jack's guidance counselor as well as with the administration. Her referral was a direct result of those conversations.

After receiving the referral form and prior to convening the initial Child Study meeting, I completed a review of Jack's school records and found some shocking information. Jack, in addition to failing the ninth grade during the previous year, had also not passed the state's standardized literacy tests, which students are expected to pass *before entering* high school and are required to pass *before graduating* from high school. He also had failed to pass *any* of the standardized End-of-Course exams administered by the state in the eighth and ninth grades, which students are required to pass in order to receive a regular high school diploma. Jack's discipline record was also extensive. We were only in the second month of the current school year, but Jack had already been in in-school suspension for 4 days and on out-of-school suspension for 4 days. No information was provided in the records about his specific offenses, but teacher reports indicated that Jack had problems with profanity, noncompliance, tardiness, and skipping classes. The records also indicated that Jack had been having behavioral problems in school since the fourth grade.

After receiving a referral on a student, I was required to schedule an initial Child Study meeting within 10 administrative days. Because this referral had been initiated at the request of the school administration, and because this student seemed to be having significant problems in school, I expected there would be an impressive turnout of school faculty and administrators at the meeting. For this reason, I was quite surprised that this Child Study meeting had to be tabled because the Assistant Principal, the parents, the school psychologist, and the referring teacher all failed to make an appearance.

Following this tabled meeting, my attempts to contact Jack's parents met with consistent failure. Jack continued to be suspended from school for various behavioral infractions. Finally, the administration required one of Jack's parents to accompany him to school for a re-entry conference before allowing him to come back to school following an out-of-school suspension. When Jack's mother came to school with him, the guidance counselor presented her with the form granting permission to evaluate Jack. Jack's mother, Ms. Shebly, signed the form without argument.

We then had 65 administrative days to complete the full evaluation on Jack and to convene an eligibility meeting. I was completely swamped with students who needed to be tested as part of their triennial evaluations, and the school psychologist, who would complete the cognitive testing component of the evaluation, was also buried in existing work. Winter break was only days away, so we decided to start Jack's evaluation first thing when we returned to school from the break.

When we returned from break, we received some absolutely shocking news. Jack's younger brother had been arrested over the break and was being held on murder charges! The story we heard was that Drew and two other teenagers had traveled out of state over the holiday and allegedly had attempted to steal money from an elderly man. When the man refused to give them any money, they allegedly overpowered him and strangled him to death with his own shoelaces, then took his money.

Jack was tremendously upset by these events, of course. He blamed himself for Drew's behaviors and stated that if he had kept a closer watch on Drew none of this would have ever happened. The school psychologist and I decided to postpone administering standardized tests to Jack, as he was too upset for the results to be valid indicators of either his ability or his achievement.

Not too long after returning to school, Jack was in trouble again and was sent to the assistant principal's office. While talking with her, he supposedly became very upset and agitated and asked her if she was afraid he was going to strangle her. The assistant principal perceived this as a threat, and Jack was suspended from school indefinitely, pending expulsion.

The school principal instructed us to proceed with the evaluation right away. However, Jack was not allowed in the school building, so we had to complete our evaluations at the county administrative building. Ms. Shebly, Jack's mother, worked two jobs and was rarely home. Jack's stepfather, Mr. Shebly, had just recently been released from prison where he had been incarcerated due to assault with a deadly weapon. Jack's stepfather was also an alcoholic. His driver's license had been revoked following several DUIs. Transportation was a major problem for Jack. The school psychologist and I spoke with Jack's stepfather several times on the telephone and arranged for Jack to come to the office building to be tested. Mr. Shebly sounded intoxicated during all of these phone conversations. The school psychologist managed to complete the cognitive evaluation. However I did not have such luck. I arranged meetings with Mr. Shebly three times and, all three times, he failed to show up. The school principal would not allow me to go to Jack's home to test him because of the stepfather's history of violent behavior. During this time, Jack placed several phone calls to the assistant principal begging her to let him come back to school and apologizing for his behavior. He also called several of his teachers just to talk with them.

We finally decided to hold an eligibility meeting without standardized educational achievement information. The information we did have included a full cognitive and psychological evaluation and sociocultural information, including a great deal of Jack's family history. The psychological data indicated that Jack had average to above average intelligence, but a considerable amount of anxiety and depression, often manifested by acting-out behaviors.

The sociocultural information shed a great deal of light on Jack's problems. A county social worker went into Jack's home and interviewed his parents. What she discovered was shocking. Jack's mother was not his real mother, and this was information Jack discovered when he was 9 years old and in the fourth grade. He and his brother had been at a local swimming pool one day during the summer

43

when they were 9 and 7 years old, respectively. While at the pool, both boys were approached by a strange woman. She told them that she was their real mother. According to bystander accounts at the time, this information obviously upset both boys. When they began to argue with the woman, she attempted to hold their heads under the water, perhaps to drown them.

In fact, Mrs. Shebly confirmed that the woman at the pool was indeed the mother of the two boys and had been a former friend of hers. She had no idea who the boy's real father was, nor did their mother. The man whom Jack and Drew had believed for years was their real father was probably not related to them at all.

According to Jack, the Shebly's home life had been tumultuous as well. He had a vivid memory of his stepfather attempting to push him out of a moving car when he was a child, and he appeared to be haunted by this memory. According to social services records, the Shebly's home had been investigated on several occasions by a social worker, but nothing was ever reported to be amiss. Jack's difficulties in school began in the fourth grade and seemed to worsen as he became older. I wonder how so many adults in the schools and in the community could have missed the obvious suffering of a child for so long.

Source: Hallahan & Kauffman (2003)

Questions About the Case
1. If Jack had been identified earlier in school as having significant problems (or a disability), how might subsequent problems have been prevented?
2. How might the teachers and school administrators have responded differently to Jack's insistence on being involved in his younger brother's behavior management?
3. If Jack's family life contributed to his problems at school, what could be done about it? How should his teacher work with him?

9. Cases on School Factors in Emotional and Behavioral Disorders

The intense, small group, individualized instruction that should be a hallmark of special education classes is lost when classes are too large. Even the best of teachers can be swamped by excessive demands. However, it is also true that some teachers make bad choices of what and how to teach students with special needs. Students may not receive the special instruction they should in a special class or resource room for a variety of reasons, as the following teacher's account illustrates. Do not be fooled into thinking that emotional and behavioral disorders do not exist among students labeled "mentally retarded" or "developmentally delayed" or some other special education category. Students with any label may exhibit highly problematic behavior, and many students in special education have multiple disabilities.

Jeremy

I haven't always enjoyed teaching children with special needs. There have been some years when my aide and I closely perused the "help wanted" section of the newspaper every afternoon after the kids left. We decided that cleaning houses, digging ditches, or washing windows from a scaffold would be less tiring and more lucrative than teaching.

We were never as stressed as we were the year Jeremy came. In the spring, all of the special classes for children with mild mental retardation were full (i.e., at or over the state limit). Some of us pleaded with administrators to open a new class for the fall. If preceding years were any indication, the system would declare a number of children in the system eligible for services after the year started. And there were always eligible students who moved into our area. But less money was available than in previous years, so salary for a new special education teacher was not in the budget.

Predictably, a new student, Jeremy, moved to our system from another state. Our supervisor asked the superintendent to sign another waiver for him to be placed in my class. He did, and Jeremy came. My class limit was 12. Jeremy was number 17.

Jeremy's educational plan was troubling. Even though he was a third grader, with an IQ score well above some of my other students, all the academic areas were categorized as "pre-readiness." Even my kindergarten students were ahead of Jeremy academically! It was clear from the information in the psychological folder that Jeremy would probably be lost in even my most delayed academic group and would require individual attention for academics.

I was fortunate to have a talented and skillful student teacher that year who took over some of my other groups so that I could devote several blocks of time to Jeremy. He soon let me know that he did not appreciate the effort! Even though I had tried to be *very* reinforcing of *any* effort on his part, he clearly was not going to go quietly to the academic trough. He whined, cried, screamed, and usually refused to participate in any instruction. I allowed him to make as many choices as possible during every lesson, reduced the length of the lessons, and increased the reinforcement. But his resistance increased. He also added verbal aggression toward me. When his mother came to observe a lesson (at my insistence), she said, "Well, *of course* he's unhappy. You're making him *do things*!"

The things I insisted he do were to trace his first name, to match four letters of the alphabet, to count objects (no more than 10). I had determined from the IEP what skills he had, planned highly structured lessons with lots of built-in choices for him, and rewarded him with objects *he* had requested (stickers, free time, stars on his papers). And he got meaner every day!

I asked his mother for a description of Jeremy's day at his previous school. There had been *no* small group or individual instruction, only whole-class instruction. His day started by finding the day on the calendar, determining the day's weather, and stating what was appropriate to wear. "They sang a lot of songs that were academically reinforcing, such as the alphabet song. Jeremy knows a *lot* of songs." Jeremy's mother had volunteered regularly in this class and was impressed with the amount of art work the children did. Every day they spent at least an hour or more (never less) on art, a half-hour exercising (even though they also had a regular gym class), and had a safety lesson.

"Mrs. Wheatley, Jeremy's teacher, also showed a lot of wonderful films and slides," she said. She went on to tell me all about the films and the picture books that the children could look at afterwards.

When I asked if Jeremy was writing on lined paper in his former school, she said, "They weren't ready to write yet."

I was angry. Here was a third grade child with an IQ of 65 who had not participated in any mainstreaming program (his class went everywhere *en masse* and separately) and had had little or no academic instruction. It wasn't that I disapproved of Mrs. Wheatley's projects. I taught the calendar, sang songs, did art, and discussed safety. I also thought it important that the children learn to write their names!

Usually, my aide, student teacher, and I switched groups often so that I could keep an eye on *all* my students. When Jeremy came, I was not as flexible. I didn't want to ask those with less training to handle a *very* difficult child. But soon, the behavior problems in the other groups made themselves known. I had 17 children and 5 reading groups, and it soon became apparent that I needed a half-hour somewhere for *another* reading group. My aide voiced my opinion: "Pat, we got too many individuals to individualize." Indeed!

Source: Kauffman & Pullen (1996, pp. 3–4)

Questions About the Case
1. How do special education teachers come to avoid effective instruction of the students in their classes?
2. What should a teacher do when class size limits or other legal or administrative requirements are waived?
3. In what specific ways did the schools and classes Jeremy attended contribute to his misbehavior?

* * * *

We must consider how disordered emotions and behavior look and feel from the perspective of the child or youth. Our conceptualizations cannot be complete until we have been able to set aside the analysis of "problem" or "disorder" from the adult's perspective and see it through the child's eyes. We can find many examples of the child's perspective in popular contemporary literature. However, consider one example of the youngster's view of school-related problems taken from the personal retrospectives of a noted special educator who worked with students who have serious problems. This special educator clearly experienced serious and painful problems of adjustment in childhood, but she was not identified as mentally ill or in need of special education.

Esther P. Rothman

From the start, I hated school, deeply, irrevocably, and silently. Kindergarten was an anathema. Rather than take me to the doctor every other day with sore throats and stomachaches that were strictly school-induced, my mother finally capitulated and let me stay at home. First grade was no better, however, and as my sore "threats" would no longer work, and as the compulsory school laws prevented my mother from withdrawing me, I had no alternative but to start off for school daily and then divert myself to the rocks and crevices that then underlay the Hellsgate Bridge in the new and growing suburb of Queens, twenty minutes away by subway from the lower East Side where I was born.

I wonder if teachers really appreciate how overwhelmingly frightening it is to be a truant. Fear possessed me completely—fear of ridicule by school-loving seat-mates, each of whom was smarter than ten of me put together; fear of God, who was certainly going to punish me by striking my parents dead; but, most of all, fear of tongue-lashings by arm-twisting teachers, who were going to debase me by "leaving me back." Which indeed they did. I was a "holdover." My teacher didn't bother to explain to my mother why I was left back, but she clearly told everyone else. I couldn't read. And I couldn't read because I played hooky—or so she said. The fact that I was already reading Hebrew and the exotic adventures of Dickie Dare in my friend Lilly's third-grade reader was totally unknown to my teacher, yet I am certain, even now, that if she had known it, she would not have altered her decision.

My teacher was what I knew she was—anti-Semitic—because my mother told me so. This was a word I learned very early in life, and I accepted it casually as I

48

accepted being an alien, one of only four Jewish children in the entire school. I felt special—not a bad feeling, but not completely good either.

I was never permitted to hold the American flag in front of the class for our morning class salute—a sacrosanct ceremony in every classroom in the entire school. My shoes were never clean enough. Once I was told I had lice. Or sometimes I did not have a handkerchief safety-pinned to the lower shoulder of my dress; this handkerchief always had to be in that exact same spot—never elsewhere. I never figured out how it was that we were supposed to blow our noses, and I never asked. I settled it myself. I had a handkerchief for showing and a handkerchief for blowing. And usually I forgot one or the other or both deliberately because I firmly believed that good little girls should never need to blow their noses at all. It was too crass. Instead, I stuffed pencil tip erasers up my nostrils. As for boys, I never even wondered what they did. Handkerchiefs were not within their generic classification.

These memories come flooding over me as I write—the hurt of being labeled a liar by a seventh-grade teacher who did not believe I had written a composition using the word *chaos* because I could not give him a definition of it. Did he never understand that I knew the word *chaos* down to my very toes because I felt it deeply every day of my life in school? Then there was the day my fifth-grade teacher threw into the garbage can the chocolate cake my mother had baked for a class party and which the children had voted to give to the teacher because it was the prettiest cake of all. And going farther back, I remember staring at the school map that hung—large, frightening, and overwhelming—from the border of the chalkboard and trying desperately to find New York State while not another child spoke—every eye, especially the teacher's, was glued to me. But worst of all was the indignity, fear, and humiliation of having to cheat on a test because I could not remember whether four-fifths equalled 80 percent.

Source: Rothman (1974, pp. 221–222)

Questions About the Case
1. What experiences described by Rothman might be similar to those of children in school today?
2. How can teachers make certain that they know what their students can actually

do?

3. How can teachers make certain that they do not discriminate against children because of their ethnic or cultural characteristics?

* * * * *

Surprises are part of teaching children with emotional or behavioral disorders, even after one has been at it for many years and become highly skilled. Mistakes and disappointments, as well as successes and gratification, are part of the territory. Special education teacher Patricia L. Pullen describes an unexpected response to a good teaching procedure with Barry, a 9-year-old youngster who exhibited a variety of problem behaviors, including failure to play appropriately with other students.

Barry

Perhaps my most frustrating and surprising experience with Barry involved an attempt to reinforce him with praise for appropriate behavior. One day as I was working with another group of children across the room I observed him playing quietly and appropriately with a classmate. Because this was something he seldom did that I wanted to encourage, I decided to do what I'd been taught will "reinforce" good behavior. I walked over to Barry, knelt beside him, gave him a hug, and commented, "Barry, I really like the way you're playing quietly with the blocks and having fun with Susie." He looked at me strangely, jumped to his feet, and screamed at me, "Well, fuck you, shitload!"

Source: Patton et al. (1991, p. 31)

Questions About the Case

1. What was Ms. Pullen trying to do in this case? Was she using an appropriate strategy?

2. If you were advising Ms. Pullen, would you suggest that she continue her attempts to improve Barry's behavior or abandon them and try something else? Why?

3. What do you see as the central problem in this case (e.g., Barry's play behavior, Barry's language, Ms. Pullen's attempt to improve Barry's behavior)?

When a teacher has success with a student whose disordered emotions and behavior have presented major problems, the gratification is enormous. Consider the sense of accomplishment the teacher must have felt in the following case.

Andy

Andy started in my class on Valentine's day. He was no Valentine. He didn't think teacher directions (e.g., "It's time to line up for lunch") were very important. When Andy wanted to play in the free-time area, he expected to be allowed to do so, and he protested loudly when he wasn't. In short, Andy wanted to do what he wanted to do when he wanted to do it without any interference from anyone, including teachers. He reminded me of a line from a Bogart movie: "I want what I want when I want it." Andy soon found out that I was not Lauren Bacall.

His teacher from the previous school in another system called me after he had been at school for two days. She was loaded with information about his family and academic information not included in the psychological folder, such as cues to give him to stop some of his undesirable behavior.

I also made a home visit. Andy's mother, Mrs. Johnson, received me in her immaculately clean dining area. She never looked at the IEP changes I wished to make in Andy's educational plan. She never looked at me. She looked at the razor strap on the table. This strap had been cut in two, had a leather thong in the top which she pulled onto her wrist. Twice, while I was there, she banged the strap on the table when one of the children was too loud or too close for her comfort. Mrs. Johnson signed the addendum to the IEP, and I left. I also vowed that Andy would get *lots* more attention from me, my aide, the principal, the speech pathologist, and anybody else I could strong-arm into doing a favor for me.

It was imperative that we get Andy in his seat, get him to stay in his seat, and to complete work that his previous teacher assured me he could do. He was fascinated with the box of shells I had collected at the beach the previous summer. I sorted them into sizes and promised him one of the tiny shells for every problem he worked correctly. I had bags and bags of shells at home that had cost me

51

nothing, and he loved them. Soon he asked, "Instead of all those little shells, how about if I get a bigger one for a whole sheet?" We discussed that the papers had to be neat, mostly correct, as well as completed. He thought that was fair. My aide found an old pencil box, covered it, and helped him glue his shells onto the box—a treasure chest. In the meantime, I sent him with good notes all over the school; to the principal, the guidance counselor, the secretary, and anybody else who expressed an interest in Andy.

Andy's work habits improved. His behavior improved. And, after a while, he began to give his shells to the younger children in the class, or back to me at the end of the day. It wasn't long before a sticker on his paper displayed on the bulletin board was enough for him.

Instead of going to the guidance counselor, principal, or secretary for stickers for his papers, he began to give his good papers to them, happy for their praise and their thanks.

The following year, he needed much less reinforcement. It seemed he was proud just to finish a paper. "I do good work, don't I?"

Source: Kauffman & Pullen (1996, p. 5)

Questions About the Case
1. What are the advantages and disadvantages of talking to other teachers about one of your students and reading the student's records before you start working with him or her?
2. What are the advantages and disadvantages of making home visits?
3. What do you see as the primary indications that the teacher was successful with Andy?

10. Cases on Cultural Factors in Emotional and Behavioral Disorders

Culture can contribute to the problems of children and youth in a variety of ways. Ordinarily, we think of culture as peculiar to a particular ethnic group. However, culture is a much broader concept than the behavior or traditions of a group identified by its ethnicity or national origins.

Teri Leigh

Teri Leigh had been removed from her home when social workers discovered that her mother's boyfriend was sexually abusing her. She and her two little brothers had been placed in separate foster homes. Her school records indicate that she has both learning disabilities and emotional disorders. She has, in fact, been diagnosed as psychotic, but I have not seen any behavior suggesting that she is having visual hallucinations or hearing voices. She is very imaginative, but I have no way of knowing whether some of the things she's reported are actually true. She is generally well behaved, but she seeks affection like a much younger child. Her affection-seeking behavior seems out of character for a 12-year-old, especially because she has a grown-up appearance for her age.

Several weeks ago, I taught the basic lesson on pregnancy and childbirth in family life class. A couple of days later, other girls in the class told me that Teri Leigh was claiming to be pregnant. I noticed that she had started bringing baby clothes to school, and there was a lot of secretive talk among Teri Leigh and the other girls. Eventually, Teri Leigh told me she thought she was pregnant. I asked her why she thought so. She explained matter-of-factly that she was probably pregnant because of what her mother's boyfriend had done to her. I explained to her several times that this was impossible because what he had done happened so long ago, but she refused to believe me.

Then I found out that Teri Leigh had given several nude photographs of herself to two high school boys who ride her bus. Luckily for us, the boys gave the pictures directly to the bus driver, who gave them to the principal, Bob Farris. When Bob called Teri Leigh's foster mother, Mrs. Overton, she told him that the pictures had been taken by Teri Leigh's foster sisters. Mrs. Overton claims that she told the girls to tear up the pictures; obviously, they had not obeyed. She refused to discuss the matter with Teri Leigh. She said that is my responsibility. Bob Farris agreed with her. So I made a stab at it.

One day I kept Teri Leigh after school and talked with her for a long time. I told her about how much I love my kids but how much time they take from me, how I have very little time for myself. I also talked to her about AIDS and other sexually transmitted diseases. Unfortunately, Teri Leigh insisted that she wants to get pregnant. And she also insisted, in spite of all the facts I gave her, that she would eventually get pregnant because of her experiences with her mother's boyfriend. I was completely unable to get through to her. What do I do now? I want to help her, but I don't know what to do next.

Source: Kauffman, Mostert, Trent, & Hallahan (1998)

Questions About the Case
1. How might biological, family, school, and cultural influences have contributed to Teri Leigh's behavior?
2. What should Teri Leigh's teacher do next? To whom should she turn for help?
3. What cultural factors make it particularly hard to address the problems of children like Teri Leigh effectively?

* * * *

Sometimes a school, a community, or a society can be considered as a case. Many people who work with individuals with problems or disabilities are concerned about the commitment of our society to those in need. Contemporary anti-tax movements severely limit the funds available to address the problems of children and families. Demographer Harold Hodgkinson made comments in the mid-1990s that still raise questions about some aspects of American culture.

The Health and Welfare of Children: How Important Are
 They in American Culture?

The Children's Defense Fund periodically reports statistics attesting to the plight of America's children, particularly those at greatest risk. In the mid-1980s, the fund's report suggested that a large percentage of American children were living in poverty and that few citizens seemed to care. In 1995, Hodgkinson made the following observations in response to the question "Who cares about America's children?"

The answer is: an astonishingly small percentage of the U.S. adult population. The demographic reasons are clear: only about one household in four has a child of school age. My conservative guess is that at least one-third of the U.S. adult population has no daily contact with a child under age 18, and the fraction could be far higher. As the median age of Americans continues to rise and as children become an even smaller percentage of the population—down from 34% in 1970 to 25% projected for 2000—the situation is likely to get even worse. People tend to vote their self-interest, and, as fewer adults have contact with children in their daily lives, there will be even less political support for programs benefiting poor children, most of whom live in central cities and rural areas while most adults live in suburbs.

Even the national leadership of groups that style themselves "pro-life" or "pro-choice" has demonstrated scant concern for the lives of the children who are *already* born. It was 30 January 1995 when the news was released that six million U.S. children under age 6 were living in poverty (up one million between 1987 and 1992) and that three-fourths of these poor children had working parents. None of the six newspapers that I checked carried the story on the front page, and two didn't even mention it. Apparently, the fact that 26% of the nation's future students, workers, voters, parents, and taxpayers have been born into the most debilitating condition of all was not deemed newsworthy. Given such a general lack of interest, it seems unlikely that there will be an increase in concern about or action in response to the amazing facts regarding poverty among America's youth. (Hodgkinson, 1995, p. 178)

Source: Hodgkinson (1995)

Questions About the Case
1. To what extent is it advantageous, and to whom, to fund government programs for the poor at low levels so that tax rates can be kept low?
2. If services for poor children are not funded by government, what are the alternatives? What does unwillingness to provide *public* funds for social service programs say about a culture?
3. To what extent can government officials be convinced to fund social service programs that require substantial expenditures in the near term but save money in the long term?

* * * *

Sometimes we do not have the courage to intervene in the misbehavior we see, partly because of our fear of being culturally insensitive and partly because we live in a culture in which much troublesome behavior is tolerated or ignored. Put yourself in the position of the writer of the following case and think about what you would have done—or what you think someone else should have done.

What Would You Have Done?

I hop on the train going toward my house and make my way past a group of kids near the door. I sit down next to a woman my age and look around me. The group of youths at the door becomes the primary focus of my attention. There are six or seven of them—one girl. I'd say they range from 10–13 years old. Two of the boys are engaged in a game of some sort, there is no distracting them. The language the others are using with each other is pretty coarse for public talk. As the train grows more full at each stop, the youth remain sprawled, as if the car were empty. New passengers step over their legs that are extended into the aisle.

Given the range of behaviors that one can reasonably expect from individuals in this age range, the kids that I can hear are skirting its edges. Perhaps for this reason, no one is issuing those warm smiles that adults so readily cast onto children. Perhaps for this reason also, a middle-aged woman, sitting just behind the group and across from me, stands up and moves to a seat farther back.

At this point, I notice the boy directly in front of me has an odd posture: almost a fetal position, slouched far, far down. New passengers walking by eye him curiously. After this happens several times, I lean forward to see what he is doing. He backs up, standing now, but hunched over—and resumes his activity of drawing on the seat in thick, dark ink. As I have obviously seen him, and he has obviously seen me see him, I must call him out—he's vandalizing a full train, after all.

"What are you doing?" I ask in a tone I think is curious but stern.

"I'm drawing [expletive.] What does it look like I'm doing?"

I freeze, redden. He looks up now. He is staring at me hard. I hold the stare, but I have no idea how to respond. He must be—what?—11.

"You can't do that," I say finally, and while we are not speaking loudly, everyone near us is taking note.

No one says anything.

"Listen, [expletive], if you don't want me to rob you, you'd better shut the [expletive] up."

"Excuse me?"

"I said, if you wanna keep your stuff, you'd better shut the [expletive] up."

This exchange goes on for one or two more rounds. I say nothing substantial. The 11-year-old continues to threaten me. I realize we have reached my stop. The woman beside me, who has obviously witnessed the entire event, stands up and says, "Excuse me," as she would normally to make her way out of our seat and off the train. I pick up my things. I can feel all eyes on me as I leave.

I have no idea what happened when I exited the train and began walking down the street. Maybe someone said or did something firm about the child's language or his action and got results. Maybe the kid kept on drawing in a car full of immobile adults while a handful of adolescents learned that intimidation is an effective means of achieving objectives.

After replaying the incident a number of times in my mind, I'm still not sure what I could have done or said to get the desired outcome, i.e. cessation of vandalism. I know my approach was not successful. I also know, for me, this event illuminated greater societal problems: that some children have experienced this kind of threatening dialogue enough times in their own lives to replicate it confidently with a stranger in public and that a group of adults allowed, for whatever reason, such an event to transpire.

Source: Contributed by Shannon Fitzsimmons

Questions About the Case
1. In what historical period do you suppose this case could have taken place? Why?
2. If you had been the narrator, how would you have resolved the situation with the youth? If you had been a bystander, what would you have done?
3. Do all students face different behavioral expectations inside and outside of the classrooms? If so, how might the discrepancies in expectation affect student behavior?
4. How does the event in this case illustrate the difficulty in distinguishing antisocial and violent behavior that demonstrates disability and such behavior that demonstrates criminality?

11. Cases on Disorders of Attention and Activity

Here is the story of a mother's two sons, John and his older brother. Both were students with attention deficit-hyperactivity disorder (ADHD). However, John had additional problems, and the story resumes in the last case included in this book.

John

I always considered myself lucky. I had grown up in a very loving family. I always wanted to get married and be a mother and wife. I got married one year out of high school and had 3 children. Then I got pregnant with a fourth child, and somehow knew things would never be the same.

My oldest and third children were delightful but very active girls, and my middle child was a boy who had been difficult to deal with behaviorally. However, he was a wonderfully bright and loving child. I sought out help early on, and eventually he was diagnosed as having attention deficit-hyperactivity disorder (ADHD). He was on Ritalin by the time he entered kindergarten and was doing quite well in school.

My pregnancy with John was pretty miserable overall because I did not feel well, either physically or psychologically. John was born 2 days before Christmas by cesarean section. So, for the first time, I had to be away from my children and husband over the holidays. In utero, John was extraordinarily active, causing me a great deal of pain and discomfort. It didn't take long to discover that he was a very different infant and child. Looking back on it, I can see now that he was born angry.

John's growth and development was relatively normal for the first couple of years. He reached his cognitive and motor milestones pretty much on target. However, he was fairly irritable and definitely hyperactive. There had been problems in my marriage before John was born, but another child with behavioral issues was the final blow. John's father and I separated when John was about 18 months old.

John's irritability and hyperactivity were so difficult to deal with during this stressful time that I took him to see a pediatrician to see whether we could get the ADHD diagnosis and put him on Ritalin. With Ritalin, we could avoid a lot of the problems I had had with his older brother, Robert. After observing John for about 4 to 5 minutes, she declared that he was a normal child and the real problem was that I wasn't coping with the break-up of my marriage. She sent us to family therapy. The general consensus at that time was that if there was a problem with a child, there was a problem with the family and with parenting techniques.

Neighbors and relatives had been quick to advise me to take a firmer hand with my boys—"Take John to the shed for a whipping a couple of times and he'll shape up," they suggested. I never believed in corporal punishment, but I did believe in setting firm limits. Indeed, I had learned a lot about parenting because of the problems I had with my older son. I read every book imaginable and went to many workshops and talks given about parenting children with behavioral problems. Many of the ideas were helpful with my other son but did little to improve things with John. My older boy was doing well enough with Ritalin, and I wanted the same for John.

I was having great difficulty keeping daycare providers for John because of his behavior. Eventually, I took John to the same place I had taken his older brother when he was finally diagnosed with ADHD. There, I met with a team of people—a couple of psychologists and a pediatric nurse practitioner—who were employed by the public school district to evaluate children in the school district who were having behavioral and learning problems. It didn't take them long to decide that John also had ADHD. Armed with their evaluation, I was able to get a different pediatrician to put John on Ritalin. The Ritalin did help somewhat, but not as much as it had helped his older brother.

Source: Contributed by Cindy Ahler

Questions About the Case

1. How are the different responses of John and his older brother to the same drug for the same problem typical?

2. How are the reactions of the neighbors and the pediatrician to the ADHD exhibited by John and his brother predictable? Why do you think school personnel were willing to see John as having ADHD when the pediatrician was not

3. If you had been John's daycare provider or his teacher in preschool, how would you have attempted to help John?

* * * *

Students with ADHD, regardless of their age, typically drive their teachers to distraction. Teachers may understand that such a child is not just the usual, active little boy (most children identified as having ADHD are boys, though it is important to recognize that girls also may have the disorder). Teachers sometimes us behavior principles very skillfully to manage ADHD. Sometimes they do not. In all cases, there is the question of whether medication is appropriate. Here is a teacher's journal, in which she records her trials and tribulations with one student.

Winnie

8/27

Well, journal, it's my first day back at school. I'm beginning my second year of teaching and I think that this time I'm in for a real treat. This year, I'll be teaching a group of "at-risk" first-graders. When my principal first asked me about this class, I wondered, "What in the world do you mean by 'at risk'?" I'd heard so many different definitions while I was in college. Well, as he explained the situation, it didn't take long for me to understand. The students I would have had been in our pre-kindergarten program, our kindergarten program, and most of them had been retained in first grade. My goodness! I had taught a class of average students last year. This year, most of my kids would be eight years old in first grade. Mr. Brown (my principal), the reading specialist, and the Chapter 1 teacher decided that instead of using the standard phonetic reading program, I'd use a basal series that combined phonetic and whole word approaches. I was also told that I should contact the consulting teacher at our school to find out about supplementary materials and behavior management techniques that I'd probably need.

9/1

Wow, it's Friday already. I haven't had time to do much writing. We've been running from one in-service program to the next all week long. Boy, these work weeks are real killers! I'll get my bulletin boards up before Monday if I work all day on Saturday and Sunday. Fortunately, Mr. Brown will be here to let us in. Oh well, such is life in the fast lane.

Betsy, the kindergarten teacher who had many of my kids last year, gave me the low-down on many of the students during lunch today. Man, I'm going to have a class full of boys—eleven of them and only three girls. Half these guys are on Ritalin. With such an active bunch, at least I don't have to worry about being bored this year!

Betsy also schooled me about one kid in particular. He's called Winnie. His real name is Winslow. He is seven years old and the only student in the class who was not retained in first grade. He's really tiny for his age, but he's also a real pistol. Betsy shared that Winnie could be so obnoxious that last year he was passed around from one kindergarten teacher to the next. She could only tolerate him for so long and then she'd have to send him to another teacher for about 30 minutes just to catch her breath. Winnie followed her everywhere—even into the bathroom. Many times she would use the class bathroom so that she wouldn't have to leave the room. The door wouldn't lock, so Winnie would just walk right in. Betsy would be sitting on the commode and he'd just walk right in.

I kid you not, Bets had me in stitches when she told me about this. She would look at Winnie with an I-can't-believe-you're-doing-this stare on her face and say, "Winnie, I'm using the bathroom." This didn't faze him in the least bit. He'd just simply respond, "But Mrs. Thompson, I have to tell you something." And then he would just say what was on his mind, turn, leave, and shut the door behind him. That's just one of the things he did all year that almost drove poor Bets crazy. I hope that knowing all this will help me cope with these problems. I'm also hoping that Winnie has matured some over the summer. Well, must get back to making the nametags for the kids. I'll try to write again soon.

11/3

My, how time flies when you're having fun! Sorry, I know it's been a while. I must be more consistent with my writing. Someday, when I'm old and gray, I'll be able to look back at these entries and have a laugh or two. For now, though, let me fill you in on how things are going.

It's now been about two months since school started, and although I'm really enjoying my class, I've already had to get some help to deal with both their academic and behavioral problems. Everybody told me at the beginning of the year that I needed to talk with Jackie, the consulting teacher at our school, for help. And so I did. Jackie has a very interesting job. Unlike us regular classroom teachers, she is not assigned to teach a group of students each day. Instead, she's available to provide consultation to those of us who have students with academic and behavioral problems. We meet with Jackie on a one-to-one basis or with a group of teachers referred to as a teacher assistance team. Frankly, I've preferred working with her on an individual basis and you know what—she's really been great! We've been meeting, planning, and implementing for only a couple of weeks, and already I can see a difference in my group.

First of all, Jackie really helped me with the reading program. It didn't take me long to realize that the basal reading program I was given to use was not the answer for my children. I mean, my kids have such limited experiences and vocabularies that they simply can't relate to the material. I needed to make reading more relevant for them. So, I talked to Jackie, and she agreed to help me supplement my reading program with a whole-language component. We're going great guns with this approach . . . .

Jackie also helped me with behavior problems. In other words, she helped me with Winnie. From the very beginning of school, he would never raise his hand. Whenever he had something to tell me, he would just blurt it out. Jackie and I talked about this, and together we came up with a plan. We decided that we would try to modify Winnie's behavior by ignoring him when he did not raise his hand and wait to be recognized. Of course, we sat Winnie down and told him what we were planning to do. To draw attention away from him, we told the class that this was something that we were doing with everyone. We expected everyone to raise their hands when they wanted to speak. Jackie did a few demonstration lessons to show me how to react to different degrees and variations of the target behavior and then I followed through with implementation of the procedure. She was—and remains—available to observe and coach me when I'm trying a new teaching strategy and this really helps me refine my skills. I really do hope this plan will work. I'm already beginning to feel the way Bets did last year.

11/19

Well, it's been two weeks since I last wrote. We've been using our B-MOD plan with Winnie and it seems that things are getting worse instead of better. You won't believe this, but as I walk around the room, he continues to call out my name constantly. If he calls my name and I don't answer him right away, he forgets what he's planning to tell me. When I finally do acknowledge him he'll say, "Mrs. Gray," and then he'll snap his fingers and go "uhh, uhh, uhh." I guess that's why he feels he has to blurt out whatever he needs or wants to say. If he keeps quiet, the poor thing knows that he is going to lose whatever's floating around in his little head. The kids have started to pick on him when he does this. I really can't afford to let things get any worse, so I'll plan to meet with Jackie and develop a modified strategy. Will try to see her tomorrow if I have the time.

11/21

Boy, it's really nice to have someone around who is so readily available. Today, I met with Jackie after school and we modified Winnie's behavior management plan. In addition to ignoring his call-outs, we also came up with a chart system for Winnie. I made a chart and divided it up into sections for reading, language, spelling, social studies, and science. If at the end of one of the blocks he hasn't blurted out an answer or called my name without acknowledgement, he'll get a plus (+). If not, if he does call out, he'll get a minus (-). If he's gotten no more than three minuses in a day's time, I'll let him do something special like read to the class. He's coming along nicely with his reading and he really enjoys showing off his skills to the rest of the class.

I know, I know. I've been bad. I said that I would write every day. Things just got so hectic after Thanksgiving that I just could not get to you. I had a wonderful Christmas! Went skiing with some friends and had an absolute blast! Got some really nice presents, too! Jerry gave me a new compact disc player. I really love the sound. Will really enjoy it.

Well, I guess I'm writing because it's getting close to that time again. On Monday, vacation will be over and I'll be back at school with my class. I'm sure Winnie will be in rare form the minute he steps off the school bus. Honestly, you'd think he'd miss a day once in a while. He's the only kid in the class who has perfect attendance!

I mentioned on November 21 that we started using a chart with Winnie. Well, before we got out for Christmas break, it finally started working to where we could get him to raise his hand before he yelled out for help or just blurted out whatever was on his mind. But you know, with all the nervous energy that this kid has, the problem just started to manifest itself in other ways. One day the psychologist came into the room to observe another student. It seems that each and every one of them has some problem or another. Anyway, Winnie raised his hand, but I didn't call on him. Well, as loudly as he could, he just slammed his hands down on his desktop. I kept on ignoring him and the longer I ignored, the louder he got. He was tapping his pencil, kicking his desk, and he continued to slam his hands against his desktop. Finally, I just looked at him and said, "I simply refuse to speak to you while you are acting this way. When you can start to act like a seven-year-old, then I'll look at you." At that point, he was really angry. He put his head on the desk and pouted. He wasn't disturbing anyone else so I just let him sit there until he cooled off.

By our last day before the start of Christmas break, I wanted to SCREAM! I just wanted to change my name because even though he was raising his hand more often, now Winnie was really into the same act that he so artfully performed in Betsy's class last year. He was constantly out of his seat, following me around everywhere I went. He followed me to the office. If I left the room to get something from another teacher I'd look back and there he was behind me. I didn't dare use the class bathroom when he was anywhere in sight. One day, he called my name so much that I just started to count the times. By the end of the day, he had called my name 37 times without raising his hand. Can you believe it? It seems like this was an improvement over his performance before we started using the chart, but he also has regressed to the point where he can never be wrong. If you tell him that he has missed two words on a spelling test—TWO WORDS—he just loses it! He bangs his head against the top of his desk, he crosses his arms and pokes out his lips, or he'll simply sit and sob incessantly. Oh, what a kid! What a kid!

I tell you about all the problems I have with Winnie, but you know, this kid is no dummy. He is the sharpest reader in my class. He can sound and blend like a champ and his comprehension is not at all bad. In math, he's a little slow with word problems, but he's great with computation and he's learning his facts with no problems. I honestly don't think that he has a learning problem. He's the youngest kid in my class, but academically, he's the strongest. Well, I'll see how he's doing in just a few days. Give me strength.

Source: Kauffman, Mostert, Trent, & Hallahan (2002, pp. 193–197)

Questions About the Case:
1. What do you see as the strengths and weaknesses of the teacher's behavior modification plan for Winnie?
2. If you were to design a plan for managing Winnie's behavior, what would be the details of your plan?
3. What are the arguments for trying medication in Winnie's case, and what are the counter-arguments?

12. Cases on Overt Conduct Disorder

Blame is easy to find in cases of conduct disorder. These are children who try the patience of their parents and teachers, often bringing out the worst in adults. However, between episodes of their disorder, they may give the appearance of being quite normal or typical, and their interactions with peers and adults may during these times be quite desirable.

Don

When I met him, he was $6^{1}/_{2}$ years of age . . . A trim four-footer, he had a sleazy look about him, like a postcard carried too long in a hip pocket. He sat in the reception room, slouched down in the chair and coolly looked me over as I approached . . . The violence of his temper outbursts was frightening and seemed to be triggered by relatively minor provocations. At school, a simple request to turn in his homework, a mild rebuke, or a suggestion that he had erred in his work could lead to shouted obscenities, overturned desks, or attacks on the other children with a pencil held as a dagger. The observers commented that in the home he ruled whatever territory he occupied . . . .

During the intervals when he was absent from home, telephone calls would often mark his progress through the neighborhood; e.g., he left school two hours early, stole candy from a store, and appropriated a toy from a neighborhood child.

No baby-sitter would brave this storm center, so the parents had long ago given up the idea of a private life, movies, or weekends together. Both parents worked. The mother (not yet 30 and physically attractive) looked as if she was in the throes of a severe illness. The family physician provided medication for her chronic depression and accompanying fatigue. Work was a reprieve from her morning and afternoon bouts with her son, Don . . . Typically, her day began at 7:00 a.m., rousing him from his wet sheets (which she changed), then scolding until he went sullenly to his tub. Once there, she washed and dried him as if he were an infant or visiting royalty.

He often dawdled while dressing, which produced a stream of prompts and commands from his mother. Suggested items of clothing were refused; this led to bitter exchanges with the now thoroughly exasperated mother. He emphasized their disagreements by kicking the door and throwing things around the room. Through all of this the mother hovered about, helping to get him dressed. She alternately cajoled and scolded, wheedled and glared.

She stood in attendance while he dined. Not only did she serve, but she finally fed him whenever he deigned to open his mouth. Through it all ran a steady cacophony of yells, cries, and arguments about whether his mother had any right to force these unreasonable requests upon him. The mother alternated between patient and antagonistic answers to his arguments and threats. At one point, she brought a stick from behind the refrigerator door. Her menacing demeanor left little doubt that she regularly employed this weapon. In the face of this ultimate threat, Don showed temporary compliance and moved forward in his glacial progress toward leaving for school.

In the afternoon Don returned from school to pick up the morning refrain. His 4-year-old brother was also available as a partner. The latter (a Machiavellian of considerable stature) knew when to probe, when to attack, and when to withdraw with tearful protestations to the protection afforded by his parents. For example, as Don sat eating his ice cream (with his fingers), the younger brother surreptitiously slipped a more efficient spoon into the mess and ran triumphantly down the hall to hide behind the door in his bedroom. Don ran shrieking after him, grabbed the door, and repeatedly slammed it into his younger brother. The screams brought both parents to the scene. The father listened for a moment to their shouted claims and counterclaims. After a brief pause, he simply began to slap both children. With that, the mother turned, walked quietly back into the kitchen and sat staring out the window.

Later the family was to go for a ride in the car. Both parents began shouting commands. In the rush of the moment, they often overlapped in their targets, e.g., the mother said, "Don, wash your face right now," while the father ordered, "Put on your jacket, Don. Hurry up now." A steady stream of commands was given as they moved toward the car. The children moved at their own pace, largely ignoring both parents.

During the day, the observers noted periods where the interactions seemed warm and positive. For example, on numerous occasions one parent would read to the children, who would often sit for long periods of time entranced with the story. At these times they seemed to be the prototypical loving family unit.

Source: Patterson (1982, pp. 294–295)

Questions About the Case:
1. Why is it easy to assume that parents do not really love their children with conduct disorder?
2. What sets children with conduct disorder apart from their peers without this disorder?
3. What suggestions would you have for parents and teachers of children like Don?

* * * *

Knowing what is the best educational environment for students whose behavior is extremely aversive to others is not simple. It demands thinking about what is best not just for the student whose conduct is unacceptable, but for other students as well.

Albert

When I observed Albert just before Christmas in the resource room where he was taught one-on-one, he was noncompliant with reasonable requests (e.g., "Sit in your chair"), and verbally and physically aggressive toward his full-time aide, his teacher, and his classmates on the playground. He had frequent tantrums, vomited and ate his vomitus, and blew his nose and wiped the mucous on others.

Albert had not started his academic life isolated in the resource room. When his parents registered him at school, they requested that Albert be fully included in the general education classroom. And even though the psychological folder from a school in another state delineated Albert's difficult behaviors, the strong medications he took every day, and his institutionalization for three months the previous year, the school agreed to the parents' request. They placed him in a second-grade class. Albert was a rising third grader, but was so small that parents and school administrators decided that he would do better in the second grade.

I was consulting in this school, and as part of this process I interviewed the teachers who were responsible for Albert's education. Mrs. Tinsley, the regular second-grade teacher, had volunteered to have Albert as part of her class. She had special education training, had fully included other children with disabilities successfully in her class, and was looking forward to Albert's coming. Her second-grade class consisted of "mostly well-behaved achieving students." Albert was coming to the Dream Team—to experienced teachers who wanted him and to classmates who would be good role models for him.

But Albert had not read the textbooks. He continued the unpleasant behaviors mentioned in the psychological folder: wiping mucous on others when his will was thwarted, screaming constantly, vomiting (once into the printer because he didn't wish to stop using the computer), pulling and grabbing the other children's clothes, and biting adults for no apparent reason other than that they were there. At first, according to Mrs. Tinsley, the other students wanted to help him. They became "big brother" or "big sister" to him. Most of the interactions his classmates initiated with him consisted of trying to cue him to comply with teacher requests, and praising him on the rare occasions when he did—just what we would have taught them to do as peer confederates.

Although a few students encouraged him to misbehave, most wanted to help him. After a while, according to Mrs. Tinsley, the students were afraid and confused by Albert's behavior. School personnel could not find strong enough rewards (or effective response cost procedures) to moderate Albert's behavior. He continued to vomit and eat it, to yell and scream. Even though all the teachers involved with Albert tried to cue him about appropriate and inappropriate comments, he still initiated conversations with classmates by asking them if they loved him or if they would marry him. He continued to pull and to grab the other children's clothing and tried to urinate on the boys when he went to the bathroom.

Albert was gradually isolated more and more in the resource room with his full-time aide. Since most of the resource students were taught in the general education classroom, Albert and his aide had the room to themselves much of the day. Even then, life was difficult, and many of the aberrant behaviors remained: the tantrums, the biting, the vomiting, and wiping his mucous on others. He added pinching to his repertoire of tortures. Albert became a despotic dictator who engaged in any and all of the aggressive behaviors mentioned if he did not get his way. The aide and teacher maintained a program of strict rules with sanctions for not complying and rewards for obeying. Gradually, the aide and teacher began to see moderate improvements in Albert's behavior. Although most of his problem behaviors did not totally disappear, Albert did establish a relationship with both the aide and the resource teacher and began to improve academically and behaviorally. Even then, he tested them periodically. The resource teacher remarked, "Just when I feel like I have a handle on this little boy, he proves me wrong."

Source: Kauffman & Pullen, 1996 (pp. 8–9)

Questions About the Case
1. How would you describe the environment that is least restrictive for a child like Albert?
2. When should the welfare of a student's classmates be weighed in choosing an educational placement?
3. If you were Albert's teacher, what strategies for reducing his noxious behaviors would you try?

13. Cases on Covert Conduct Disorder

Children with covert antisocial behavior often exhibit overt antisocial behavior as well. In fact, multiple problems are more the norm than are isolated problems. George is a case in point.

George

George's first-grade teacher, Mrs. Anderson, came to the child study meeting concerned about his behavior, which was frightening her and her other students. George was highly noncompliant, aggressive, and abusive to himself and others. Some teachers thought George should have a full evaluation immediately, but an administrator demanded prereferral strategies in Mrs. Anderson's class. Mrs. Anderson was visibly upset, even though she was given a list of strategies recommended by "experts."

Mrs. Anderson faithfully followed the strategies and documented the results for two weeks. George was no better. She described George's daily fights with his classmates. She also told the child study committee how George had stolen a tooth from another child's backpack in an attempt to get a reward from the "tooth fairy." After he was told that if he lost one of his own teeth he would get the reward, but not if he stole someone else's tooth, George put a block in his mouth, chomped hard on it, broke his tooth, and demanded a reward. The school nurse corroborated the story.

The administrator who had demanded prereferral strategies maintained that the female teachers were overreacting, that George was just a normal, active little boy. However, George's fighting, cursing, and stealing increased in spite of the best efforts of the teachers. In fact, his behavior got worse. Mrs. Anderson refused to plead his case before the child study committee anymore. "What does it take to get you people to refer a student? Murder? Suicide?"

George stomped the innards out of a dead bird one day on the playground. He cackled and laughed while stomping. He hit a teacher who tried to stop him from throwing rocks at other kids on the playground. And his teacher told others that one day he stroked her breast and said, "This'll be our secret. Don't tell anyone, and we can do it again."

The final act that got George referred was hanging from a railing around open steps to the basement level of the school. Had he lost his grip, he likely would have been very seriously injured or killed. He was finally referred, found eligible for special education, and placed in a special class for students with emotional disturbance. The class was on the second floor of the school, and George made repeated attempts to jump out of the window. After being moved to another school with only one floor, he tried repeatedly to run away, and his violence escalated.

Source: Kauffman & Pullen (1996)

Questions About the Case
1. What might have been done to prevent George's increasingly troublesome behavior?
2. If George were your student, what would be your primary objective? Why?
3. What suggestions would you have given Mrs. Anderson for prereferral interventions?

* * * *

Children and youth who steal, lie, or exhibit other covert antisocial behavior may carry a variety of labels. They may be considered mentally retarded, learning disabled, or gifted. The common thread among them is their sneaky, unacceptable behavior that puts them at odds with others, both their peers and adults in roles of authority.

Timothy

Timothy began his second-grade year in my class for students with mild mental retardation. He was tall for his age (8). His smile, complete with dimples, was heart-melting, and he had large brown eyes. I thought that he was one of the most physically appealing children I had ever taught. He also learned quickly—too quickly for a child with cognitive problems, and after a few months I insisted that he be reevaluated.

At first, the support teachers, the librarian, the music teacher, and the physical education teacher all thought he was a precious child. Or, as the librarian said, "Precious and precocious." However, the honeymoon was short-lived, and Timothy began to torment the students in my class and those in the regular classroom. Mr. Allan, the gym teacher, escorted him back to my room one day and said, "The other children in the class have been complaining about Timothy always picking on them, but until today, I never caught him at it. Here's the bent paper clip that he's been sticking children with." He handed me a paper clip that was redesigned to hurt.

When I informed the instructional assistant that Timothy had found a paper clip and used it as a weapon in gym, she said, "Patty, we're missing almost a whole box of paper clips. Maybe we'd better ask Timothy if he can find them."

Timothy politely complied when we asked him to empty his backpack on the table, but protested loudly when about 30 paper clips hit the table. "Somebody put those in my backpack. I swear to God, I never took your paper clips!"

Later, my aide said, "There are other supplies missing, Patty. We'd better watch him."

That afternoon, I visited Timothy's mother, Mrs. Agnor, and asked permission to mark all of Timothy's possessions with a small dot with a magic marker. I also asked her if we could make a list of everything that Timothy had in his backpack every morning, including snacks and lunch. I explained to Timothy and his mother that either the instructional assistant or I would check his desk and backpack several times during the day, and if we found items that did not have a dot on them or were not on the list he would have to return the items and lose some of his free time. Mrs. Agnor asked me to call her immediately if we found any stolen items. I agreed.

For about a week, Timothy had no unmarked or unlisted items, and I was feeling good about the plan his mother and I had implemented. Then one morning I found a fancy pencil, an eraser, and a plastic ring, all of which resembled things from my "treat box" (the box in which I kept things to give my students as rewards or treats for good work). When I asked him where he had gotten those things, he said, "People give me things. Other teachers give me stuff." My aide and I listed and marked all his items, including the treats.

Several mornings after that, Timothy had prizes that I suspected came from my supply; however, when I discussed this with my aide, we both wondered how Timothy could reach the box of treats, which was on the top shelf of the closet. We had to use a step stool and stand on our tip-toes to reach them. We also wondered *when* he could steal. Every morning, he participated in the breakfast program, which I supervised, and when he finished breakfast he went to the regular class for homeroom. According to his homeroom teacher, he was never late.

One morning, a kindergarten student walked into the corner of a table for the third time that week, and when I comforted him he said, "Well, why you all time movin' that ol' table?"

My aide and I realized that the table was a bit off kilter every morning, and both of us had assumed that the custodian had moved the table when he cleaned. But my aide said, "Isn't it puzzling that all of the other tables in this big room are always where we leave them in the afternoon? Seems just that one is always out of place."

When I spoke with Timothy, I gently held his right hand and placed my other hand on his chest. I said, "Timothy, you have been stealing from me, and after we have a talk, I'm going to call your mother. I want all of my treats returned."

"No ma'am, I didn't take those things. How am I gonna get up on the top shelf of that closet? Tell me that!"

"Okay, while we were on duty, you opened the closet door, pulled the table over to the closet, stood on the table, took what you wanted, put the box back, and then dragged the table back."

He looked scared, and I thought for a moment that he was going to cry. "I'm sorry. I won't steal from you again."

A few days later, a new student registered in my class. Brian was a handful, and on his second day in my class he threw an eraser at another student and hit him in the back of the head. I asked Brian to accompany me in the hall so that we could have a private chat. On the way out the door, Timothy murmured, "Man, don't let her touch your chest. Just don't let her touch your chest."

That's when my aide and I realized that Timothy was in awe of my right hand, which he assumed had the power to discern lies and read minds. We never told him otherwise.

Source: Case contributed by Patricia L. Pullen

Questions About the Case:
1. In what ways did Ms. Pullen follow acceptable or suggested procedures for dealing with youngsters who steal?
2. Supposing that Ms. Pullen had not been able to figure out how Timothy was stealing, what would have been the consequences or outcome for Timothy?
3. What alternative ways of confronting Timothy about his stealing could you suggest?

14. Cases on Special Problems of Adolescence

These three brief cases should be considered together.

V. K.

V. K., a teenager serving a 15-year sentence for the second-degree murder of a 16-year-old classmate, will not have her sentence reduced. She was a 15-year-old senior when she became involved in a knife fight with another student at a school bus stop. Testimony in her trial indicated that dozens of students and adults stood by without intervening as the two fought. The girl who was stabbed bled to death from a wound in her neck, one of several she received in the fight.

Scarface

The child, nicknamed Scarface because of the cuts and scars on his face, was 10 years old, only 5 feet tall, and weighed just 90 pounds. He was accused of molesting a 10-year-old girl on school grounds while one of his friends held her down. The judge released him into the custody of his parents. Over the next 10 weeks, he was arrested 5 more times—more times than any other juvenile in Washington, DC, in that year. His other arrests were for holding up and robbing two men, threatening a woman with an iron pipe, participating in a brawl, illegally entering a car, and assaulting a woman and stealing her purse.

Sammy

Sammy was identified as eligible for special education services when he was in the first grade. In addition to qualifying for services under the category of emotional and behavioral disorders, he was found to have mild to moderate mental retardation. When Sammy was 15, he was picked up by the police at 10:00 P.M. for questioning regarding a burglary at a local clothing store. After an hour of questioning without his parents or an attorney, Sammy indicated that he knew something about a killing at a convenience store in town earlier that year. Sammy waived his right to an attorney and proceeded with the interrogation without notifying his parents. He eventually confessed to being the trigger man in the shooting. Although the details of his story did not fit the facts of the case, Sammy was tried as an adult and, based on his own confession, convicted and sentenced to more than 50 years in prison. The irony in this case is that Sammy was considered to be unable to meet the standards for a high school diploma in the state of Virginia (based on a series of minimum competency tests), but he was considered competent to understand the decision to waive his rights to an attorney during his interrogation.

Sources: Newspaper reports and personal experiences

Questions About the Cases
1. Should any of these students be considered adults in the justice system?
2. Under what conditions would you not hold people legally responsible for their behavior?
3. Under what circumstances would you consider onlookers who did not become involved or participants equally as guilty as the individual who did a criminal or antisocial act?

* * * *

The problems of adolescents often involve acting-out behavior, better known as conduct disorder. Often acting-out in school is accompanied by or followed by other serious problems involving delinquency, sexual behavior, or substance abuse.

Matt

Matt is a seventh grader who attends a modified self-contained classroom for students with "serious emotional disturbance." However, he is included in a regular homeroom and goes to lunch with his regular classroom peers.

In his regular homeroom, Matt is prone to jump onto a desk and, when asked to get down, leap from desk to desk proclaiming loudly "You can't catch me!" He may then fling himself upon a student below. On one occasion he rigged the wiring of his homeroom's overhead projector such that someone touching the metal casing would receive an electrical shock. His prank was reported to the teacher by another student before anyone was hurt.

He has torn down the entire ceiling of the restroom, destroyed fixtures, and started fires in the restroom, although he is escorted to and from the restroom by a female aide. His inability to handle unstructured time in his homeroom and unsupervised activities elsewhere in the school is a contrast to his successes in the highly structured special class.

Source: Kauffman, Lloyd, Baker, & Riedel (1995)

Questions About the Case:
1. How would you describe the prognosis for student like Matt?
2. Were you advising his teachers (both special and general educators), what suggestions would you offer?
3. How would you respond to someone's suggestion that Matt needs to be with his regular classroom peers so that he can learn appropriate behavior?

* * * *

We too often forget than many adolescents make it through difficult times, that they are resilient in ways that many of us can hardly imagine. Corwin (1997) provides richly descriptive, fascinating stories of how adolescents in environments in which they saw gangs, delinquent behavior, substance abuse, and early sexual experience did not succumb, at least not to all young people and not to all of the negative pressures in their lives. In some ways and at some times, nearly all adolescents exhibit problem behavior. In many instances, they overcome the negative influences of their environments or are able to correct their problem behavior. Teachers, both general and special, may be positive influences on adolescents' behavior.

Latisha

Latisha demonstrates her excellent writing in an AP English class, but her oral language is that of the impoverished East Lost Angeles, a kind of "ghettoese." She wears her hair in dyed-blond cornrows. She tells her teacher that reading James Joyce's *Portrait of the Artist As a Young Man* was heartrending for her, as it reminded her a lot of her own messed-up family. She has been struggling with her own history.

She grew up in a housing project with her mother, brother, and her mother's boyfriend. She attended elementary school in Huntsville with mostly middle-class white students. She was not part of the gifted program until she was allowed to take a special IQ test and, to the amazement of her teacher, made it into the gifted program.

Reading Joyce prompted her to recall her sexual abuse by her mother's boyfriend, starting when she was eight and continuing until she was in the fourth grade. Due to the sexual abuse, she became angry, hostile, and withdrawn, started fights with other children, and let her grades slip.

Although Latisha's mother broke up with her boyfriend and so the sexual abuse stopped when Latisha was in the fourth grade, her mother then began using crack cocaine and left Latisha and her brother alone for days at a time. When her mother was home, she physically abused Latisha, who started wearing long sleeved shirts to school to cover her injuries. When she was in the eighth grade, relatives sent her to live with her father in Los Angeles because they considered it safer for her. Her father had no room for her, so she lived with an aunt, who put her to work cleaning her house and babysitting.

In high school, Latisha was lonely and started drinking, often bringing gin and juice to school in the morning. She was an alcoholic at the age of fifteen. Her early sexual abuse haunts her.

Willie

Willie is six feet four inches tall. He has a full beard and a diamond earring. He gives the impression of being in his mid-twenties, but he is just a large and gifted high school senior. He is a popular student who has been active in student government since ninth grade and is taking several honors classes.

In an essay written for an AP English class, he reveals much that his teacher did not know. His family was stable until it was destroyed by his mother's drug (crack cocaine) dependency. He watched her go to prison. His father, a Vietnam vet who worked for the postal service, encouraged him to be successful in school and never missed a parent-teacher conference. His friends envy his relationship with his father. But Willie often felt alone, abandoned by everyone.

Willie's mother was released from jail, but immediately went back on drugs. He saw her on the front lawn, disheveled and disoriented. Seeing her this way made him cry, as he loved and missed his mother.

After considering going to Pepperdine University (near Los Angeles) on a scholarship, he decided, much to the dismay of his father, to attend Morehouse College in Atlanta. Eventually, his father approved of his decision.

In their high school, Willie was elected homecoming king and Latisha was homecoming queen. Few of the students who elected them knew what these two students had lived through.

Source: Corwin (1997, Chapter 19)

Questions About the Cases:
1. Why did Latisha become an alcoholic but Willie did not become a substance abuser?
2. Had you been Latisha's or Willie's teacher in elementary school, what could you have done to help improve their lives?
3. Supposing you had been Latisha's or Willie's high school AP English teacher, what are the things you could have done to help them most?

15. Cases on Anxiety and Related Disorders

Kane's personal description gives us a small window into the experience of one person with Tourette's Syndrome (TS, also known as Tourette's disorder) and the way it is related to internal states. The experience of TS, like the experience of any other disorder, is highly individualized. However, the attentional and obsessive-compulsive aspects of TS appear to be common themes in people's first-person accounts.

Kane

I experienced TS onset 19 years ago, at age 7. My first symptom was head jerking, and subsequent (primarily simple tic) symptoms included facial tics, extremity tics, vocal tics (e.g., squeaking, grunting), and touching tics. From ages 11 to 13, I was prescribed haloperidol, but eventually, because of side effects, I was prescribed clonidine. One year later, clonidine was deemed ineffective and all medication was discontinued.

Perhaps the best description for the sensory state of TS is a somatic hyperattention: It is not as itch-like as it is an enduring somatosensory bombardment. I experience the TS state as one of keen bodily awareness, or a continual consciousness of muscle, joint, and skin sensations . . . If all tics are suppressed, virtually all of my joints and muscles begin to demand my attention. The TS state heightens to a stiffening feeling, such that my skin feels like a hardened casing and my joints feel as though they are becoming rigid. The intensity rises until it becomes so unpleasant and distracting that tics must be executed (with a compulsion that rivals the scratching of a severe itch).

The reason that tics are only marginally effective in providing relief, however, is that unlike scratching an itch, tics do not make the hyperattention go away. Tics merely reset the TS state temporarily back to a baseline. Thus, tics are not themselves pleasant, but they do provide a temporary respite from the persistent hyperawareness.

Source: Kane (1994)

Questions About the Case:
1. If you had a student in your class who began showing stereotyped movements, what should be your response (i.e., what should you do, how should you handle it)?
2. How would you describe the relationship between TS and attention problems?
3. How could you best show understanding and support for a student with TS?

* * * *

We ordinarily think about special schools as having particular value for students with acting-out behavior. However, special classes and special schools can also provide environments where students with internalizing disorders feel safe and can flower.

Pauline

Pauline entered the school bedraggled. Tall and slender, she hobbled in more like a wounded crow than a graceful swan. This was Pauline's first day in a special school for students with emotional and behavioral difficulties. She was now 14 years old.

For the past 3 years in secondary school, her life had been a story of daily trauma. Due to her height, she had very quickly become the butt of jokes among her peer group. The jokes led to bullying—verbal taunts and eventually physical attacks. Teachers tried to intervene, but always the hunting pack of students would seek out its prey, and Pauline would again fall victim to abuse from her peers.

Pauline changed from being an outward-going student of average ability, always eager to contribute in class. She became withdrawn, pale, shoulders hunched, and frightened to speak or to be spoken to for fear of ridicule. When teachers unaware of the peer pressure she was suffering urged her to play a more active role in class, she became distraught. School was no longer a safe place; Pauline began to play truant. When her parents discovered this, they forced her to attend school daily by taking her there themselves. This caused Pauline physical distress to the extent that she would vomit. Her peer group turned on her even more, barring her from entering the bathroom when she needed to be sick (pretending, if a teacher passed by, to be helping her).

Pauline's emotional state did not cause her to display aggressive behavior, but it certainly reflected a disturbed child who found her whole school environment disturbing and alien. Such was her mental state that she began to underachieve in all lessons. There were suggestions from teachers that she had specific learning difficulties. She was certainly suffering from curriculum malnourishment. The curriculum diet she was receiving was failing to give her any sustenance. She was failing to thrive in her school environment, merely existing as a lonely, hyper-anxious, vulnerable child. She had lost her dignity.

At the instigation of the educational psychologist, an alternative placement was sought in a special school for students with emotional and behavioral difficulties. As the weeks passed in the special school, Pauline began to make contact with the teachers. She would never speak in class, but after a lesson ended, she would hang around to discuss some point with the teacher. Teachers were soon convinced that she did not have any significant learning difficulty.

Her attendance was good. Gradually, the dreadful pallor began to fade; her eyes lost some of their traumatized glare. She eventually shared with the school counselor the extent of her personal pain and anguish over the previous three years. She described it as "a daily nightmare." She had found the secondary school of 1,500 students totally disorientating. Once her peer group abandoned her, she described herself as "floating in a sea of people," none of whom she recognized, or who recognized her.

In the small special school of 40 students, Pauline found peace. She learned to trust again—first adults, and then fellow students. She became an active participant in classroom learning experiences, no longer the peripheral onlooker. Her capacity to care for others became clear, and she befriended many isolated individuals.

Her time at the special school was short. She left at the age of 16, and not all problems had been solved by far. Three years of lost education cannot be regained in two. New situations or change still caused Pauline anxiety. But when she left the school, she had a renewed sense of self-worth. This "restrictive environment" had been her safe haven; it had given her back her dignity.

Source: Carpenter & Bovair (1996, pp. 6–8)

Questions About the Case
1. How would you respond to someone's argument that Pauline belonged in a regular class in a regular school, not the special school?
2. If you were a teacher in a regular school, how would you respond to bullying of students like Pauline?
3. What would be required to make all schools small, supportive, and inviting places for students like Pauline?

16. Cases on Depression and Suicide

Sometimes it is difficult to understand the discomfort of depression because it seems unreasonable to us. Children, youth, or even adults who are depressed may seem to others to have a completely irrational view of the world and to be frightened of things that are extremely unlikely to happen.

Bryan

Bryan is a 10-year-old boy who manifests many of the signs of childhood depression. He expresses sadness, social withdrawal, disinterest in sports, and increasing complaints of stomach aches. Over the past 10 weeks, Bryan has become increasingly disinterested in his studies. Although he continues to display excellent scores on standardized achievement tests, he has been receiving failing grades in many subject areas. His grades began deteriorating immediately after his father and mother separated. The separation resulted after a protracted period of conflict between his parents that ultimately included both verbal and physical aggression. During the interval that immediately preceded the separation, the parents admit to being preoccupied and had little inclination to interact with Bryan. Both parents have experienced depression in the past, and Bryan's mother is currently involved in therapy and receiving antidepressants. Bryan believes that he is at fault for his parents' separation and that there is little hope for a reconciliation between his parents. Although his father visits him on a weekly basis, Bryan is afraid that each visit is the last and that he will never see his father again.

Source: Stark et al. (1995, p. 277)

Questions About the Case
1. In what ways is Bryan's case typical of children experiencing depression?
2. What do you think were the primary causal factors contributing to Bryan's depression?
3. Supposing that you were Bryan's teacher, how would you have responded (what would you have done) to deal most effectively with his anxiety and depression?

Teachers may find themselves working with depressed or suicidal students without anticipating problems. Too often, problems are ignored until they become undeniable and very dramatic.

Pat

Pat is a fifth-grade girl who is at or above grade level in all academic areas. However, she has been highly oppositional and defiant of all teachers since kindergarten. Large for her age and strong, she pushes, hits, and threatens her peers, who are fearful of her and will not initiate any interaction with her. She sometimes bangs her head on her desk or the floor, shouting, "I'm no good!" or "I want to die!" Pat was evaluated for special education only after terrorizing her classmates and a substitute teacher by tying the cord of a classroom window blind around her neck and jumping from a table, bringing the blinds crashing down with her in an apparent suicide gesture.

Source: Kauffman, Lloyd, Baker, & Riedel (1995)

Questions About the Case:
1. What do you see as the essence of Pat's problems?
2. If Pat's problem behavior were to have been prevented, what would have been required (at various ages or grades)?
3. Given Pat's behavior, what suggestions do you have for her teacher?

17. Cases on Severe Mental Disorders

Wanda was diagnosed with childhood schizophrenia and reported having auditory hallucinations—hearing buildings and other objects talk to her. Excessive fantasies can make a student very difficult to teach, if not inaccessible to teaching. Note the frustration of Wanda's teacher.

Wanda

I was aware, of course, that emotionally disturbed children sometimes have wild fantasies, but I was not prepared for Wanda. Wanda was 11 years old when I met her. She had a tested IQ of about 160, but it didn't do her much good except, perhaps, to enrich her fantasy life. I was never able to find a topic of conversation, an area of the curriculum, a place, or a time that was free of her bizarre imaginings. She had fantasies about jeans—she "wore" special 40-pocket and 100-pocket jeans with zippers in the front and drew stylized pictures of them. She had fantasies about the president and the governor and crucifixes and *The Pit and the Pendulum*, doctors, nurses, swimming pools, toilets, injections, physical examinations . . . , moles (she had one on her arm that was a microphone into which she talked and one on her leg that was a thermostat controlling her body temperature) . . . . [T]here was no end.

When she engaged in her fantasies, Wanda got a peculiar, fixed grin on her face, her eyes became glazed, she giggled, and she talked (often apparently to herself) in a high-pitched squeaky voice. Frequently, she drew pictures with captions representing fantasized objects and activities. Sometimes she engaged in other bizarre behaviors, such as flattening herself on the floor or wall, kissing it, caressing it, and talking to it. It was impossible to teach Wanda or to have a rational conversation with her while she was fantasizing, and she was "in" fantasy most of the time. It was impossible to predict when, during times of lucidity and reality-oriented behavior, she would suddenly enter her fantasy world again.

Source: Patton et al. (1991, pp. 29–30)

Questions About the Case:
1. How was Wanda typical and how was she not typical of children diagnosed with schizophrenia?
2. If you were Wanda's teacher, how would you respond to her fantasies?
3. If you were going to intervene to prevent or control Wanda's fantasies, how would you try to do so?

* * * *

Sometimes children eventually diagnosed with schizophrenia are first diagnosed with other problems. And sometimes medication and special education are very helpful in coping with schizophrenia.

Bill

Bill's difficulties began during infancy. He was described as a colicky baby who was in constant motion and prone to head banging. During early childhood he required constant supervision because of his high activity level, unpredictable behavior, and tendencies toward destructive behavior such as hurting family pets and lighting fires. Because of delayed visual-motor functioning, Bill was placed in a school for children with learning disabilities at 6 years of age.

Bill's behavior became increasingly bizarre. He began to defecate and urinate in odd places, would scratch and hit himself, and threw himself against the walls crying. He became preoccupied with germs, death, and sex, and would panic if separated from his mother. At roughly 8 years of age, Bill's language became illogical and difficult to follow and tended to drift to morbid themes. At home and at school Bill acted as if he was hallucinating. During one episode he claimed that blood was oozing from the walls and floors and frantically attempted to tear them apart. He began playing with knives, talked of killing himself, and jumped off a high roof. Bill showed increasing signs of depression, spent his time lying on the sofa, and talked about hating himself.

Concerns about suicidal behavior and deteriorating behavior led to Bill's psychiatric hospitalization. A trial of haloperidol was initiated and his behavior stabilized with the combination of medication and the structured inpatient treatment program. After roughly 2 months of inpatient care, Bill returned home where he received outpatient therapy, continued on haloperidol, and attended a school program with a highly structured behavioral program and considerable individual attention. His special education classroom contained eight students, and classroom work was supplemented with daily individual tutoring.

Until age 13, Bill continued to be described as highly anxious and as sometimes disorganized, out of touch with reality, bizarre, and silly. He showed persistent problems with attention, unpredictable mood changes, impulsivity, and daydreaming. These difficulties were most apparent during unstructured times, and the structure of the behavioral program appeared to help him control his behavior. Despite his difficulties, Bill was described as likable, popular with classmates and teachers, intelligent, and curious.

Bill showed gradual but steady improvement. At age 15 he was taken off haloperidol with no adverse effects. He transferred to his neighborhood high school, received A's and B's in his classes, and was described as a boy who "liked to study and apply himself." He developed a group of friends and became active in sports and school activities. At the final interview, when Bill was 17 years old, he was described as a popular high school senior, editor of the school newspaper, and a member of the soccer team. The summer before his senior year, he had held a responsible job working in his father's business. There were no signs of schizophrenia or other psychiatric disorder, and Bill was preparing for college the following year.

Source: Asarnow et al. (1994, pp. 610–611)

Questions About the Case:
1. Why do you think Bill's schizophrenia was not recognized immediately?
2. Had you been Bill's teacher in the early grades, what action would you have taken to address his problems?
3. In what ways is Bill's case typical and in what ways is it not typical of childhood schizophrenia?

Elizabeth was diagnosed with schizophrenia as a child. Her case was introduced in the earlier section on conceptual models (Chapter 4). Here, she gives us a first-person description of what the experience is like.

Elizabeth (continued from case on biogenic conceptual model)

I certainly heard voices. They started in the fourth grade when I was really sick. At first the voices were friendly; then they got mean and scared me to pieces. I got so I couldn't even go into my bedroom because I was so scared that a voice who lived there might get me. Then for a while some other voices came, and they were good voices who protected me from the bad voices. The good voices were the first to disappear when I started taking medicine, and then I just had to be frightened of the bad voices again.

It was 6 years ago that this happened, so I really don't remember what the voices said to me. But I do remember that it was a very bad experience. I always had a terrible headache when the voices came, so the doctors x-rayed my head to see if they could find anything wrong with my brain, but there was nothing wrong.

When I was sickest, I could even see the voices. They were very weird. They were like ghosts (one of them had three heads). When I was in the hospital, I drew pictures of them and some even had names like "Greenie." I have wallpaper in my bedroom of old-fashioned girls with bonnets, and it used to seem to me that they would come alive and come off the walls to attack me, which was pretty scary.

My psychiatrist said I shouldn't spend any time thinking about the voices. Whenever I felt a voice attack coming on, I would go to my mother. She could always tell I was in trouble because I would get big, dark circles under my eyes. She would say "Distract," and she would make me lie down and relax. It worked.

Now the voices seem like a bad dream. I don't ever, ever want them to come back. Schizophrenia is a very painful disease.

Once while I was in the hospital, the voices told me to jump out of the window. But I didn't want to because I was afraid of heights (I was on the sixth floor). I told my nurse about this and I was put within constant sight. I had to sleep in two chairs pushed together next to the nurse's station.

Source: (Anonymous, 1994, p. 589)

Questions About the Case:
1. In what ways does Elizabeth's case illustrate the pain of having schizophrenia?
2. Why is schizophrenia often not recognized immediately in children?
3. Had you been Elizabeth's teacher at some point in her life, what could you have done that would have been most helpful?

18. Final Case

You should recall the beginning of this case in the chapter (11) presented for disorders of attention and activity. John's mother briefly describes her expectations, John's siblings, and the problem of ADHD in the earlier part of her story. Here, she takes up the development and management of additional problems.

John (continued from case on attention and activity disorders)

John's birthday is in December, so he entered kindergarten just shy of his sixth birthday. He went to the same private K–8 elementary school that his older siblings had attended. His teacher was older than most and very exacting. At the end of the year she decided it would be better for him if I kept him in kindergarten another year because of his behavior, even though he was functioning at grade level academically. I chose not to do this because I felt his self-esteem would suffer. The next year, his first-grade teacher was enthusiastic but not very experienced. She believed that he was not capable of keeping up with the other students academically and that he did have difficulty with peer relationships. According to national standards, John's skills were still at grade level. However, at this school most of the children operated substantially above grade level, which placed him near the bottom of his class. She would not pass him on to the next grade, and the principal stood behind her decision. I decided that rather than keeping him back I would send him to public school.

The local public school was very different from the private school. He had a second-grade teacher who could not control her classroom at all. At the end of that year, according to the standardized tests, John had not gained any ground in his reading and math skills and so was a year behind where he should have been. I returned him to his former school the following year. There, the new principal assured me that we could all work together and achieve success for John.

John started third grade with new resolve. Early on, I attempted to form a partnership with his teacher to help John be successful. However, she made it abundantly clear to me that at this age she expected John to remember to go get his medications at lunch time and to copy down and do his assignments without prompting from her. She told me the only way to get him to act responsibly was to hold high expectations and punish him when he failed to meet those expectations. John was still having difficulty with peer relationships as well. He was very small for his age and looked immature. He had a very hot temper. The other children teased him endlessly, and he was frequently in trouble for fighting. One day on the playground, two children were teasing him and he swung his backpack at them. His teacher saw him do it. During homeroom period, she took him out into the hallway and slapped him across the face, nearly knocking him over. This was witnessed by several of his fellow classmates, and I only heard about it later when several parents called to tell me. Their own children had come home from school and were very upset about their teacher's behavior. Since there were only a couple of weeks left in the school year, I kept him home and did school work with him there.

The next year I was able to petition to get him into a different public school, one that was known for working well with children with ADHD. He did struggle, but he did relatively well that year despite some new problems. At this time, John was discovered to have a deficiency in growth hormone and began having daily growth hormone injections. Over the course of this year, there were weeks at a time when he would be a virtual recluse. He would come home from school, turn off all the lights, close the drapes, and sit two feet from the TV, almost in a trance. He was particularly irritable at these times, and if friends called to ask him to come out and play he wouldn't even talk to them on the phone. He had difficulty getting to sleep at night, and he was difficult to get up for school in the morning. Eventually, he began to tell me how much he wanted to die because he hated his life. He began displaying some self-injurious behavior. We consulted a child psychiatrist, and John was eventually admitted to the children's mental health unit at the local hospital. They tried some anticonvulsant medications (then the standard treatment for bipolar disorder), and his mood and behavior began to improve. Then he developed a severe allergic reaction to the drug he was taking and to other medications in that drug category. The psychiatrist would not diagnose bipolar disorder, which both John's pediatrician and I now suspected was his problem. Instead, the psychiatrist diagnosed him as having Oppositional Defiant Disorder (ODD) and ADHD. The psychiatrist told me that I simply could not allow John to behave this way and had to set firmer limits on his behavior. I must make John be responsible for his own behavior. He said I was looking for the "magic" pill and there wasn't one.

In the fall of the next academic year, on one of the few occasions when he played outside, he jumped out of a tree about 20 feet off the ground and shattered his ankle. This required surgery to repair and casting that lasted three months. His behavior began to take on a different pattern. In the fall and spring he had periods when he was extremely hyperactive and displayed a volatile temper. Then in the winter he would be reclusive, generally irritable, and very emotional, with multiple episodes of uncontrollable sobbing. It was during these times that he would do things to injure himself. His endocrinologist thought he might have a seasonal affective disorder. Then John's behavior pattern changed again. The periods of time with depressive-like symptoms and the hyperactivity seemed to occur both during the winter and spring, which would be inconsistent with seasonal affective disorder.

At the end of sixth grade, John's teachers passed him on despite the fact that he really was non-functional in school. They told me that he needed to get into a special education program especially designed for children with behavioral problems.

He went to the public junior high in the fall and was placed in a special education program. In this program, there were children who had behavior problems, but they were all very different problems from John. Many had been in trouble with the law. They had stolen cars, vandalized property, were truant from school, or had been in trouble with illegal drugs. Most had significant problems in their families. In order to fit in with the group, John had to become more like them. He began to be disrespectful to me, curse and swear, and be much more defiant to authority figures. When we found medications that would adequately quiet John, he became so sleepy that he couldn't stay awake at school. If we didn't medicate him, he became volatile and was locked in the school's "time-out" room, which was basically a padded cell. We endured two more years of this. As before, he was passed to the next grade, even though he was getting next to nothing out of school.

The junior high experience was also very isolating for John socially. I couldn't let him visit any of his friends from school at their homes because the environments were so bad. He was allowed to bring friends home, but his friends stole some of John's prized possessions. John was crushed and didn't understand this. Of course his behavior was too strange even for them, and they would beat him up. He had to learn to put on a very tough exterior and become even more like them just to survive.

Senior high was even worse than junior high. That is when I began to realize that John was smoking marijuana and suspected there were other illegal drugs involved. School authorities expected more from him. They actually held the special education students to a much higher standard of behavior than the mainstream students. There were a million ways to get suspended from school, and John must have found at least half of them. In ninth grade, he spent more time suspended than he did attending school. More often than not, the school would only inform me of the suspension by mail several days after the fact rather than at the time it happened. In other words, he would be out running around during the day and I would think he was in school. It was during one of these many school suspensions that John jumped off the top of a bus stop and severely fractured both of the bones in his forearm. Life was constant turmoil.

This senior high school also had a policeman assigned to the school full-time. Whenever there was a possibility to get the law involved, the school did. It became very clear to me that John was being warehoused in a school system that had no idea what to do except call the police. They didn't want these children, and the consensus was that if these children could not behave properly the teachers or administrators would find a way to have them locked up and sent away.
So, I decided to move out to a rural area. I was convinced that getting John out of the city and away from the influence of the gang members who were his classmates was crucial. We moved about 40 miles out of the city to a neighboring rural county and were able to get a mental health case manager through this county almost immediately (John had been on a waiting list for three years in the county in which we had lived previously). I do believe this social worker tried hard to be helpful, but I soon realized how limited those services were. She was able to get some assistance from an agency that provided after-school home care. By this time John's mood swings were very wide, with frequent fluctuations. I also found the kids in John's special education program were not very different from the inner city setting, except that they didn't belong to gangs. John quickly

became acquainted with drug-using friends. Actually, the drug-use problem in this rural county was far worse than in the large metropolitan school.

Within a very short time, the school staff decided that John was simply not able to function in a classroom for very long periods of time. It was decided that he should attend school half days. Every day when John got home from school, he was supposed to sit down with the after-school caregiver and do homework. The irony was that even though he couldn't sit still in school, the after-school caregivers believed they could make him do it at home. It was a constant battle, and he was forever being sanctioned for one thing or another. John had a volatile temper but he had never been violent to others. Mainly, he would scream and curse, trash his own belongings or his room, or do something to injure himself. He would attempt to leave, and the caregivers would call the police to have him picked up as a runaway who might harm himself. At school, the assistant principal tried to have John arrested for "assault with a deadly weapon" because he threw a paper clip across the room in the direction of one of his teachers. The paper clip hit the blackboard, but not the teacher.

The assistant principal decided that next year John should not be in a classroom with other children. She was convinced that his behavior was attention-seeking. She isolated him by placing him in a room with an aide who was to give him his schoolwork to do. The aide was there to watch him, keep him on track, and assist him if he had questions. He was not allowed to go to the lunch room or to interact with any of the other students attending the high school. His behavior became more and more bizarre. One minute he would be bouncing off the lockers that were in that room, and the next minute he would be rolling around on the floor crying. It became clear to me that he was "rapid cycling" from manic to depressed, then repeating this cycle, all in a matter of minutes. Still, the psychiatrists never witnessed these episodes and therefore would not diagnose bipolar disorder. At this point he was on Lithium and Ritalin, but it was clear that they were not working well for John.

Eventually, John was expelled from that school. The school administrators felt he was a danger to himself and others. I had him schooled at home by a tutor for the remaining weeks of the school year. The teacher came to our home six hours per week. She was very good with John, and he did make some progress. She was willing to allow him to walk around during their lessons, and he was actually able to get some schoolwork done that way. Still, it was woefully inadequate.

The next year, the local school district had set up a special school program for kids who had not been successful in the usual EBD programs. John's mental health case manager thought John would be appropriate for this program. They had a psychologist, in addition to the regular teaching staff, who would be there every day and spend time with each of the children daily. Additionally, John's county mental health case manager would be a frequent and regular visitor to the school.

The school psychologist and the county case manager became alarmed one day because John had burned and cut himself. The case manager came to our house and attempted to get my insurance to hospitalize him as injurious to himself. But the insurance company would not authorize it unless John stated that he was going to kill himself or someone else. John no longer felt that way.

A few weeks later, the psychologist became convinced that John was using drugs and was chemically dependent. The psychologist decided to appeal to my insurance company to give him a chemical dependency assessment. They agreed to have him hospitalized for a day or two for a chemical use evaluation. When I brought him there, the hospital staff was convinced he was on something. John denied this, and I was sure that he had not had the recent opportunity to obtain any drugs. Nevertheless, the staff confronted him on this. I am not sure exactly what happened after that, but John became very volatile, and the staff placed him in seclusion, where he went totally out of control and became psychotic. The staff called the psychiatrist from the psychiatric ward to come and deal with him.

The psychiatrist ordered a dose of Haldol which quickly calmed him down. John spent a great deal of time talking with the psychiatrist. For the first time John admitted to hearing and seeing things. He said that the last medicine he was given made him feel calmer and think more clearly. The psychiatrist called me and explained that John had been admitted to the psych ward and explained what had happened. The psychiatrist told me that he thought John was in acute mania. I told him that if he thought that was acute he should have seen him during the previous month, because I thought the mania was beginning to subside when I brought him in. The psychiatrist told me that he would like to put him on a different medication, similar to Haldol but with less severe side effects. John developed a severe allergic reaction to the first medication they tried but was placed on a different medication in the same "atypical antipsychotic" drug class. John really did seem much better on this medication, and for the first time I felt there was some hope for the future.

The psychiatrist told me and the rest of the care team that it was clear to him that I had spent considerable time with John trying to reach him and help him to learn proper behavior. It had never mattered before that I had successfully raised three productive children before John. I was always blamed as one of the factors in John's behavior problems. Now that John was able to think more clearly, he was able to reiterate what behaviors were expected of him. However, the challenge would be that he was nearly 18 years old and had spent the last 10 years developing secondary behaviors in his attempt to cope with his mental illness and psychosis and now needed to eliminate these behaviors. Additionally, since John was so young when the beginning signs of his mental illness emerged, his social and emotional development was halted at a 3- to 4-year-old level. No one had any clear idea about how to help him catch up in his social and emotional development. But at least now we had the diagnosis that I thought would help people to understand and stop blaming him and me for the behavior and really begin to help him. I was soon to find out how wrong that assumption was.

During all these years, the stress had been nearly unbearable, and it was affecting my physical health. At the time John was discharged from the hospital, I was admitted to the hospital and had my sixth abdominal surgery. I was discharged from the hospital after 3 days, and the next day was visited by the county case manager and the psychologist from John's school. They had decided to drop him from the program, and now it was determined he should go to the ALC (Alternative Learning Center) once per week to pick up assignments and then work at home on his own. I knew this would never work. I told them how incredibly unfair this was because he was not even given a chance to learn how to adapt and change since getting on better medications. But they had already made up their minds. He was discharged from the program, and someone else filled his spot just that quickly.

After leaving that program, I was able to get John into an in-patient state mental health hospital program. They had a psychiatrist on staff who actually spent time with my son more than once per week. She diagnosed John as "schizo-affective bipolar." This program was the best I had seen to date, and John did get a lot out of the program. It was more successful than others because they incorporated a behavior modification program that gave real incentives for desired behavior but was not so punitive for undesirable behavior. When children exhibited undesirable behavior, they did not lose all the credit they had built up with good behavior, but were simply not able to earn merit points for a set period of time. Unfortunately, that program was time-limited, and John was discharged back home to me about 4 months later.

John spent the next three years trying to complete his high school diploma on a new IEP, all while I was attempting to help him further his social and emotional development. With little to no help from the school or county, I pushed and prodded John until he was able to meet the goals set out by the IEP and get his high school diploma by the time he turned 21. Nevertheless, to this day he is barely literate and has few job skills. Currently, his social and emotional development is about that of a 15-year-old, which makes it incredibly difficult. People expect him to act his chronological age. Progress is occurring, but when it is two steps forward and one step backward it is very discouraging. I have been attempting unsuccessfully for the past year to get John in an assisted living situation because I no longer feel he is making progress living with me and I need some relief before my health really fails me.

Source: Contributed by Cindy Ahler

Questions About the Case
1. How would you respond to suggestions that John's mother caused her son John to have emotional or behavioral disorders?
2. What role, if any, do you think teachers had in John's problems?
3. How, if at all, do you see cultural factors as causing or contributing to John's problems?
4. What would lead you to the conclusion that John's problems were primarily a result of biological factors?

5. Imagine that at some point in the story told by John's mother you were John's teacher. What would have been the most important and helpful things you could have done as his teacher?

References

Anonymous. (1994). First person account: Schizophrenia with childhood onset. *Schizophrenia Bulletin, 20,* 587–590.

Asarnow, J. R., Tompson, M. C., & Goldstein, M. J. (1994). Childhood-onset schizophrenia: A follow-up study. *Schizophrenia Bulletin, 20,* 599–617.

Berkowitz, P. H. (1974). Pearl H. Berkowitz. In J. M. Kauffman & C. D. Lewis (Eds.), *Teaching children with behavior disorders: Personal perspectives* (pp. 24–49). Upper Saddle River, NJ: Merrill/Prentice Hall.

Carlson, P. (2003, January 26). The psychotic bank robber: A schizophrenic teen takes desperate measures. His parents want help. The law wants prison. *Washington Post,* F1, F4–F5.

Carpenter, B., & Bovair, K. (1996). Learning with dignity: Educational opportunities for students with emotional and behavioral difficulties. *Canadian Journal of Special Education, 11*(1), 6–16.

Corwin, M. (1997). *And still we rise: The trials and triumphs of twelve gifted inner-city students.* New York: Perennial.

Dunlap, G., Robbins, F. R., & Kern, L. (1994). Some characteristics of nonaversive intervention for severe behavior problems. In E. Schopler & G. B. Mesibov (Eds.), *Behavioral issues in autism* (pp. 227–245). New York: Plenum.

Goor, M. B., & Santos, K. E. (2002). *To think like a teacher: Cases for special education interns and novice teachers.* Boston: Allyn & Bacon.

Hallahan, D. P., & Kauffman, J. M. (2003). *Casebook to Accompany Exceptional learners: Introduction to special education* (9th ed.). Boston: Allyn & Bacon.

Hodgkinson, H. L. (1995). What should we call people? Race, class, and the census for 2000. *Phi Delta Kappan, 77*, 173–179.

James, M., & Long, N. (1992). Looking beyond behavior and seeing my needs: A red flag interview. *Journal of Emotional and Behavioral Problems, 1*(2), 35–38.

Kamps, D. M., Leonard, B. R., Dugan, E. P., Boland, B., & Greenwood, C. R. (1991). The use of ecobehavioral assessment to identify naturally occurring effective procedures in classrooms serving students with autism and other developmental disabilities. *Journal of Behavioral Education, 1*, 367–397.

Kane, M. J. (1994). Premonitory urges as "attentional tics" in Tourette's syndrome. *Journal of the American Academy of Child and Adolescent Psychiatry, 33*, 805–808.

Kaslow, N. J., Morris, M. K., & Rehm, L. P. (1998). Childhood depression. In R. J. Morris & T. R. Kratochwill (Eds.), *The practice of child therapy* (3rd ed., pp. 48–90). Boston: Allyn & Bacon.

Kauffman, J. M., Lloyd, J. W., Baker, J., & Riedel, T. M. (1995). Inclusion of all students with emotional or behavioral disorders? Let's think again. *Phi Delta Kappan, 76*, 542–546.

Kauffman, J. M., Mostert, M. P., Trent, S. C., & Hallahan, D. P. (1998). *Managing classroom behavior: A reflective case-based approach* (2nd ed.). Boston: Allyn & Bacon.

Kauffman, J. M., Mostert, M. P., Trent, S. C., & Hallahan, D. P. (2002). *Managing classroom behavior: A reflective case-based approach* (3rd ed.). Boston: Allyn & Bacon.

Kauffman, J. M., & Pullen, P. L. (1996). Eight myths about special education. *Focus on Exceptional Children, 28*(5), 1–12.

McHugh, J. (1987, April 5). Portrait of trouble: Teen's crimes began early. *Daily Progress,* pp. A1, A6

Maruskin-Mott, J. (1986). Portrait of Mark Matthews. *Gifted/Creative/Talented, 9*(6), 53.

Mayo, T. (1839). *Elements of pathology of the human mind.* Philadelphia: Waldie.

Noll, M. B., Kamps, D., & Seaborn, C. F. (1993). Prereferral intervention for students with emotional or behavioral risks: Use of a behavioral consultation model. *Journal of Emotional and Behavioral Disorders, 1,* 203–214.

Patton, J. R., Blackbourn, J. M., Kauffman, J. M., & Brown, G. B. (1991). *Exceptional children in focus* (5th ed.). Upper Saddle River, NJ: Merrill/Prentice Hall.

Patterson, G. R. (1982). *Coercive family process.* Eugene, OR: Castalia.

Rappaport, M. M., & Rappaport, H. (1975). The other half of the expectancy equation: Pygmalion. *Journal of Educational Psychology, 67,* 531–536.

Rappaport, S. R. (1976). Sheldon R. Rappaport. In J. M. Kauffman & D. P. Hallahan (Eds.), *Teaching children with learning disabilities: Personal perspectives* (pp. 344–371). Columbus, OH: Charles E. Merrill.

Rothman, E. P. (1974). Esther P. Rothman. In J. M. Kauffman & C. D. Lewis (Eds.), *Teaching children with behavior disorders: Personal perspectives* (pp. 218–239). Upper Saddle River, NJ: Merrill/Prentice Hall.

Serbin, L. A., Stack, D. M., Schwartzman, A. E., Cooperman, J., Bentley, V., Saltaris, C., & Ledingham, J. E. (2002). A longitudinal study of aggressive and withdrawn children into adulthood: Patterns of parenting and risk to offspring. In R. J. McMahon & R. D. Peters (Eds.), *The effects of parental dysfunction on children* (pp. 43–69). New York: Kluwer.

Stark, K. D., Ostrander, R., Kurowski, C. A., Swearer, S., & Bowen, B. (1995). Affective and mood disorders. In M. Hersen & R. T. Ammerman (Eds.), *Advanced abnormal child psychology* (pp. 253–282). Hillsdale, NJ: Erlbaum.

Thomas, A., Chess, S., & Birch, H. G. (1968). *Temperament and behavior disorders in children*. New York: New York University Press.